MW00893605

Islam
and
Christianity

Islam and Christianity

Brothers at Odds

Second Edition

Odeh A. Muhawesh

Odeh Muhawesh is a graduate of the Global Institute for Islamic Studies where he earned his Ph.D. in comparative theology. He is the author of numerous books and essays on matters of world religions and the history of religious development. Dr. Muhawesh is an adjunct professor of theology at the University of St. Thomas where he teaches history of the modern Middle East and Islam. He is a regular speaker at churches, synagogues, colleges, and universities around the nation. Currently, he is chairman and CEO of TruScribe and serves on several boards including the board of advisors of the College of Arts and Sciences, the William C. Norris Institute, and the Muslim-Christian Dialogue Center, and he is a special advisor to the Jay Phillips Center for Interfaith Learning. Dr. Muhawesh is an expert on matters of interfaith dialogue, world religions, foreign affairs, and national and global business leadership and ethics.

© 2017 by Unity Publishing, LLC.
All rights reserved. Published 2017.
Printed in the United States of America

ISBN-13: 978-1-977-66760-1

No part of this publication may be reproduced without permission, except in cases of fair use. Brief quotations, especially for the purpose of propagating Islamic teachings, are allowed.

Contents

Preface

Islam is the world's fastest growing religion. Fifty-seven countries across four continents hold majority Muslim populations. In addition, there are significant Muslim populations in many non-Muslim majority countries such as Russia, China, many African countries, and several member countries of the European Union.

While most human segments are declining in population due to various factors, Muslims are growing in number and are becoming progressively younger. According to the article Demographic Trends in Muslim Countries:

> Putting the population growth of Muslim-majority countries in a global perspective, the Middle East and North Africa (MENA) region has the largest concentration of countries with populations that are more than 90 percent Muslim. The region experienced rapid mortality decline during the second half of the 20th century, while fertility remained relatively high. As a result, between 1950 and 2000, the MENA region experienced the fastest population growth among the world's major regions. MENA's population growth reached a peak of 3 percent per year around 1980, while the growth rate for the world reached its peak of 2 percent annual growth more than a decade earlier.

Considering where most Muslim-majority countries are in their demographic transition—most Muslim-majority countries (plus Nigeria) still have fertility rates above the world average of 2.4 children per woman. Islam may indeed remain the fastest-growing religion in the world for the foreseeable future.[1]

At the same time, non-Muslim populations are slowing in numbers and aging at a faster pace.

Researchers writing in the journal Science said European population growth reached a turning point in the year 2000 when the number of children dropped to a level that statistically assured there will be fewer parents in the next generation than there are in the current generation.[2]

In effect, the momentum for population growth in the 15-nation European Union has flipped from positive to negative, and that trend could strongly influence population numbers throughout the twenty-first century. This population decline in non-Muslim countries is not limited to Europe. Many other countries are declining due to myriad factors.

A number of nations today, stretching from North Asia (Japan) through Eastern Europe, including Ukraine, Belarus, Moldova, Estonia, Latvia, Lithuania, Bulgaria, Georgia, Armenia, and into Central and Western Europe, including Bosnia, Croatia, Serbia, Slovenia, Germany, Hungary, and now Greece, Italy and Portugal, along with Puerto Rico in the Caribbean, now face long-term population decline. Countries rapidly approaching long-term population declines (but currently still growing, albeit slowly) include Greece, Spain, Cuba, Uruguay, Denmark, Finland, and Austria. Russia is also facing long-term population

1. Farzaneh Roudi-Fahimi, John F. May, and Allyson C. Lynch, "Demographic Trends in Muslim Countries," Population Reference Bureau, April 2013, accessed January 2016, http://www.prb.org/Publications/Articles/2013/demographics-muslims.aspx.
2. Bootie Cosgrove-Mather, "European Birth Rate Declines," CBS News, March 27, 2003, accessed 2015, http://www.cbsnews.com/news/european-birth-rate-declines/.

decline, although for the moment there has been a reversal due to an increased birth rate.[3]

_____▲_____

Many nations in Europe today would have declining populations if it were not for international immigration. The total population of the continent of Europe (including Russia and other non-EU countries) peaked around the year 2000 and has been falling since 2004.[4]

Declining populations have great impacts on many factors of human society. For example, aging populations are less productive and exit labor forces much faster. They are also less likely to be interested in investing in research and development initiatives, which adversely affects future development and advancement of nations. Conversely, younger populations are the future labor force of world economies and have more interest in new inventions and advancement as well as political change.

Taking Europe as an example, an aging European population and declining birth rate forces European countries to rely on immigrant workers to sustain their economies. When examining the options for available migrant labor it becomes readily apparent that North Africa and the Middle East are the natural and most economical sources for such force. This fact manifests itself in the large Muslim immigrant populations of Europe, with France having five million Muslims and Germany with four million Muslim immigrants. One can conclude that Muslims by and large constitute the world's future labor force.

The Middle East and North African region (MENA) is geographically vital to world trade since most of the maritime shipping lines and air and land routes pass through it. One manifest example is the Suez Canal that connects the Mediterranean with the Red Sea through

_____

3. Wikipedia, The Free Encyclopedia, s.v. "Population Decline," accessed February 15, 2015, https://en.wikipedia.org/wiki/Population_decline
4. Population Press. n.d., accessed 2015, http://www.populationpress.org/publication/2004-1-myers.html.

Egypt, thus it is the only maritime passage connecting Europe and North America to the Indian Ocean and the Far East, unless shippers travel around the southern horn of Africa. This would significantly increase the cost of shipping and durability of products and cause significant delays and costs of product exchange between Eastern and Western economies. Middle Eastern natural resources have established importance in world economies. Today, 60% of the world's crude oil is found in the Middle East, the heart of the Muslim world.

Understanding Islam and its teachings and the history of its followers is vitally important for academics, politicians, journalists, and all stakeholders in the future of our world. I wrote this book a number of years ago as I spoke to or engaged in dialogue with non-Muslim westerners. My goal is to give non-Muslims and Muslims alike a way to understand Islam beyond the usual simplified narrative that primarily focuses on rituals and some Islamic beliefs. I start off in chapter one with the accounts of Adam's creation and Eve's creation in the Bible and Quran. If you would like to read a primer on Islam before you read this book, I discuss the main beliefs and practices of Islam and a brief history of Islam in the appendices.

While I discuss contemporary issues like war, I also cover more fundamental matters such as the story of the creation of Adam and Eve, angels versus jinn, and similarities between Islam and Catholicism. I made an effort to educate the reader on issues related to Islam with an eye on comparing those issues with Christianity—specifically to highlight the intricate relationship between not only Muslims and Christians but also Islam and Christianity. I have studied both faiths for tens of years and have come to the undeniable conclusion that Islam and Christianity are brothers at odds, and, thus, I believe that Muslims and Christians should be brothers and sisters in *salam*—peace and harmony.

······•◆•······

Chapter One

The Accounts of Adam and Eve

Although many similarities exist in the story of creation between Islam and the Judeo-Christian tradition, vastly different outlooks exist between them. We will begin by examining the account of Adam and Eve according to the Old Testament followed by an examination of the same story from the Quran.

The Account of Adam and Eve in the Old Testament

The creation of Adam and Eve

For Christians, the story of creation begins in the Book of Genesis. In Genesis, it states that God created Adam. Then He created Eve from Adam's rib in order to be a companion to and subservient to Adam. Eve was named by Adam.

------------------------▼------------------------

And the LORD God said, "It is not good that man should be alone; I will make him a helper comparable to him." Out of the ground the LORD God formed every beast of the field and every bird of the air, and brought them to Adam to see what he would call them. And whatever Adam called each living creature, that was its name. So Adam gave names to all cattle, to the birds of the air, and to every beast of the field. But for Adam there was not found a helper comparable to him. And the Lord God caused a deep sleep to fall on Adam, and he slept; and He took one of his ribs, and closed up the flesh in its place. Then the rib which the Lord God had taken from man He made into a woman, and He brought her to the man. (Genesis 2:18–22)

Consequences of the story for women

This account of Adam and Eve's creation has the potential to be viewed as demeaning to women. In this depiction, women are placed in the same class as cattle and birds, a class that was created by God but named by Adam. According to the Book of Genesis, Eve is then tempted by the forbidden tree. She is the first to fall to the deception of the serpent.

So when the woman saw that the tree was good for food, that it was pleasant to the eyes, and a tree desirable to make one wise, she took of its fruit and ate. She also gave to her husband with her, and he ate. (Genesis 3:6)

It is indeed remarkable to have Eve fall to the deception of the serpent first. The serpent, being the manifestation of all evil, does not attempt to deceive Adam but focuses on the weaker being, Eve. The story tells of a being who is ready to violate God's law willingly and easily for self-interest. Eve, after all, was willing and easily persuaded by the serpent to eat from the forbidden tree.

In the Biblical account of the event, Adam did not blame the serpent for tempting him to eat from the tree. The account places the blame squarely on Eve who tempted Adam to eat from the tree. This depiction leads the reader to interpret Eve and the serpent as equally guilty of the action and, thus, of causing humanity to fall. Whereas Adam is portrayed as a blameful victim in the Biblical story, Eve was the willing participant in violating God's law.

In fact, the wording in Genesis allows Adam to imply that God was to blame for the event. Adam said to God when He asked him how Adam knew he was naked by responding, "The woman whom You gave to be with me, she gave me of the tree, and I ate" (Genesis 3:12).

There is an implication that Adam was not even willing to call her by the name that he gave to her, for in the Biblical Adam's view, she was forced upon him by God.

Remarkably, the Bible states that God did not argue with Adam but quickly directed His anger at "the woman" and the serpent. Genesis depicts the cursing of the serpent, then relates every hardship Eve endured for her willingness to go along with the serpent. As for Adam, he is then punished for heeding the voice of his wife:

Then to Adam He said, "Because you have heeded the voice of your wife, and have eaten from the tree of which I commanded you, saying, 'You shall not eat of it.'" (Genesis 3:17)

This aspect of the story is sometimes understood as a command to husbands not to heed the "voices of their wives." Applying this interpretation in today's world would mean that women should have no opinion in important matters and consulting them on decision-making would be a violation of Biblical wisdom. However, for Adam, and therefore for men, this may even lead to the idea that any decisions made based on a woman's opinion could cause them great suffering.

Christianity's leading thinkers cite Genesis as the cause for the oppression women faced in western Christendom. According to Christopher L. C. E. Witcombe:

▼

For the last two thousand years or so, Eve has represented the fundamental character and identity of all women. Through Eve's words and actions, the true nature of women was revealed; her story tells men what women are really like.

Eve represents everything about a woman a man should guard against. In both form and symbol, Eve <u>is</u> woman, and <u>because</u> of her, the prevalent belief in the West has been that all women are by nature disobedient, guileless, weak-willed, prone to temptation and evil, disloyal, untrustworthy, deceitful, seductive, and motivated in their thoughts and behaviour purely by self-interest.

No matter what women might achieve in the world, the message of Genesis warns men not to trust them, and women not to trust themselves or each other. Whoever she might be and whatever her accomplishments, no woman can escape being identified with Eve, or being identified as her.

In the West, the story of Eve has served over the centuries as the principal document in support of measures and laws to curtail and limit the actions, rights, and status of women. The Pseudo-St. Paul, for example, in his Pastoral Epistle to St. Timothy, could cite Genesis as the reason why women should not be allowed to teach or to tell a man what to do:

> For I do not allow woman to teach, or to exercise authority over men; but she is to keep silent. For Adam was formed first, then Eve. And Adam was not deceived, but the woman was deceived and became a transgressor. (1 Timothy 2:12–14)

The early Christian theologian Tertullian (c. 155/160–220 CE), reminded women that they all share Eve's "ignominy . . . of original sin and the odium of being the cause of the fall of the human race":

> Do you not believe that you are (each) an Eve? The sentence of God on this sex of yours lives on even in our times and

4

so it is necessary that the guilt should live on, also. You are the one who opened the door to the Devil, you are the one who first plucked the fruit of the forbidden tree, you are the first who deserted the divine law; you are the one who persuaded him whom the Devil was not strong enough to attack. All too easily you destroyed the image of God, man. Because of your desert, that is, death, even the Son of God had to die. (The Apparel of Women, Book I, Chapt. 1)

During the Middle Ages, St. Bernard of Clairvaux could claim in his sermons, without contradiction, that Eve was "the original cause of all evil, whose disgrace has come down to all other women." This perception of Eve has endured with remarkable tenacity and persists today as a major stumbling block in attempts by women to correct gender-based inequalities between the sexes. Consciously or unconsciously, it continues to serve as the ultimate weapon against women who wish to challenge male hegemony.[5,6]

Consequences of the story for humanity

Another remarkable aspect of the Biblical narrative is that Adam and Eve were expelled from heaven for having gained knowledge of right and wrong:

Then the LORD God said, "Behold, the man has become like one of Us, to know good and evil. And now, lest he put out his hand and take also of the tree of life, and eat, and live forever. . .therefore the LORD God sent him out from the

5. Christopher L.C.E. Witcombe, "Eve and the Identity of Women," accessed February 2015, http://witcombe.sbc.edu/eve-women/.
6. An earlier version of this essay appeared originally in Images of Women in Ancient Art, http://www.arthistory.sbc.edu/imageswomen/.

garden of Eden, to cultivate the ground from which he was taken. (Genesis 3:22–23)

A reasonable question is then raised. Why would God levy such heavy punishment on humanity for gaining knowledge? How can we, the children of Adam and Eve, know and love God if it is not through knowledge? Further, does this indicate that they did not know of good and evil before eating from the tree and thus, they should have not been punished for eating from it?

It was based on the story of Eve's tempting of Adam and her haste to obey the serpent, for which humanity was sent down from the garden to suffer on Earth, that Saint Augustine formulated the doctrine of original sin. In his Confessions, Augustine of Hippo writes:

I sought to know what wickedness was, and found it was no substance, but a perverse distortion of the will away from the highest substance and towards the lowest things; the will casts forth its innermost part and swells outwards.

The enemy kept his hold on my powers of willing, and had made of it a chain for me, and bound me with it. My will was perverted, and became a lust; I obeyed my lust as a slave, and it became a habit; I failed to resist my habit, and it became a need...my two wills, the old, carnal will, and the new, spiritual will, were at war with one another, and in their discord rent my soul in pieces.

Therefore it was no longer I that did this, but the sin that dwelt in me—that sin itself being part of the punishment for a sin more willingly committed, since I was a son of Adam.[7]

The human presence on Earth, then, is punishment for the sin committed by Eve, with Adam as an accomplice. This justifies God's

---

7. Augustine of Hippo, *The Confessions of Saint Augustine*, (New York: Signet, 1963).

supposed anger with humanity and His demand for repayment for the betrayal of Adam and Eve. In this account, God sent many prophets to Adam and Eve's children in an attempt to return them to the right path. They, in turn, betrayed the prophets one after another, until God finally abandoned His efforts to set humanity right and sent His son (Jesus Christ) to be sacrificed to satisfy God's demand for repayment.

The Account of Adam and Eve in the Quran

The account of Adam and Eve is mentioned in several places in the Quran. The Islamic holy book is topically arranged, unlike the Bible which is chronologically structured. The first encounter of the account of God's creation of Adam and Eve is in chapter two of the Quran:

When your Lord said to the angels, "Indeed I am going to set a viceroy on the earth," they said, "Will You set in it someone who will cause corruption in it, and shed blood, while we celebrate Your praise and proclaim Your sanctity?" He said, "Indeed I know what you do not know." And He taught Adam the Names, all of them; then presented them to the angels and said, "Tell me the names of these, if you are truthful." They said, "Immaculate are You! We have no knowledge except what You have taught us. Indeed You are the All-knowing, the All-wise." He said, "O Adam, inform them of their names," and when he had informed them of their names, He said, "Did I not tell you that I indeed know the Unseen in the heavens and the earth, and that I know whatever you disclose and whatever you were concealing?" And when We said to the angels, "Prostrate before Adam," they prostrated, but not Iblis: he refused and acted arrogantly, and he was one of the faithless. We said, "O Adam, dwell with your mate in paradise, and eat thereof freely whencesoever you wish; but do not approach this tree, lest you should be among the wrongdoers." Then Satan caused them to stumble from it, and he dislodged

7

them from what they were in; and We said, "Get down, being enemies of one another! On the earth shall be your abode and sustenance for a time." Then Adam received certain words from his Lord, and He turned to him clemently. Indeed He is the All-clement, the All-merciful. We said, "Get down from it, all together! Yet, should any guidance come to you from Me, those who follow My guidance shall have no fear, nor shall they grieve. But those who are faithless and deny Our signs, they shall be the inmates of the Fire and they shall remain in it [forever]. (Quran 2:30–39)

▲

Humans as representatives of God on Earth

In this first encounter, God tells of His decree to assign a representative on Earth who will have complete dominion therein. The angels, wanting this lofty position for themselves, present their case to God for being worthy of this position. They were aware that the purpose of such assignment is to represent God on Earth so they pleaded that their glorification and praise of God is the ultimate form of worship— therefore they are worthy of this assignment.

God then pointed out to them that Adam was given knowledge they did not possess, and, therefore, he was more worthy of this position. This knowledge of the "names" of certain individuals who would come from Adam throughout the ages made the angels submit in prostration to Adam immediately. These individuals whose names Adam knew, indicating that he knew their importance and identity, are believed to be the prophets and their successors from Adam until the end of time. God chose them not only to guide humanity but also to know and worship Him as the one and only God.

Lucifer disobeys God

Upon submission by the angels and, therefore, all other creatures, to humanity for having dominion over Earth, one certain creature refused to accept humanity's role as viceroy of God. When God asked this creature, whose names in Arabic and English respectively are Iblis and Lucifer, about the reason for his refusal to obey God's command, Lucifer replied, "You made me of fire and you made him of clay."

This statement is believed to have been the very first sin committed against God. The sin of arrogance and racism overcame Lucifer. Lucifer argued that because he was created before Adam and was made of what he believed to be a mightier substance, fire, he would not submit to him, whom he believed was an inferior being made from clay.

Certainly We have established you on the earth, and made in it [various] means of livelihood for you. Little do you thank. Certainly We created you, then We formed you, then We said to the angels, "Prostrate before Adam." So they [all] prostrated, but not Iblis: he was not among those who prostrated. Said He, "What prevented you from prostrating, when I commanded you?" "I am better than him," he said. "You created me from fire and You created him from clay." (Quran 7:10–12)

The Quran continues to reveal that God condemned Lucifer for refusing to accept human dominion over Earth:

"Get down from it!" He said. "It is not for you to be arrogant therein. Begone! You are indeed among the degraded ones." (Quran 7:13)

God grants Lucifer respite

Lucifer was since damned by God and deemed not worthy of being in paradise.[8] However, due to God's justice, he asked God not to expedite his expulsion from this world into the eternal damnation of the hereafter, and God granted his request:

> He said, "Give me respite, until the Day they are resurrected." He said, "You are of those given respite; until the marked day." (Quran 7:14–15)

A question often asked by many is why God would grant Lucifer's request to delay his death and punishment until the end of times. The answer could be found in Muslim traditions which state that Lucifer (Satan) was created many years before the creation of Adam and during those many years he prayed to God once. Because God is just, He would not condemn even Satan without rewarding him first for that one prayer. This aspect of the story is sometimes used to show the importance of every good deed no matter how small it may appear, for if God delayed the punishment of the worst devil for such a long time, then the reward for anyone who performs good deeds can only be immeasurable.

It is worth mentioning that God did not grant Satan's request to live until the Day of Resurrection, rather He delayed his demise until the "marked day." This marked day is believed to be when Prophet Muhammad shall slaughter Satan in Jerusalem after the second coming of Jesus, many years before the end of time.[9]

---

8. In the Quran, Lucifer is referred to as "the satan" after he is expelled from the garden.
9. Quran 15:38 and 38:81

The creation of Eve

Returning to the account of the creation of Adam and Eve, we notice that Eve appeared on the scene as Adam's mate, but little reference is given in the Quran to where she came from. The only references we can cite from the Quran are those which state that both Adam and Eve were created from the same soul:

O mankind! Be wary of your Lord who created you from a single soul, and created its mate from it, and, from the two of them, scattered numerous men and women. Be wary of Allah, in whose Name you adjure one another, and the wombs. Indeed Allah is watchful over you. (Quran 4:1)

In addition, in chapter 7 of the Quran, God states:

It is He who created you from a single soul, and made from it its mate, that he might find comfort with her. So when he had covered her, she bore a light burden and passed [some time] with it. When she had grown heavy, they both invoked Allah, their Lord: "If You give us a healthy [child], we will be surely grateful." (Quran 7:189)

This latter verse indicates that Adam and Eve were created from one soul and that comfort is the natural state of the relationship between Adam and Eve, and, therefore, between men and women, as they were created from one soul. It is further notable that Eve's pregnancy is not viewed as punishment for eating from the forbidden tree but as a sign of the comfort that exists between the two genders.

Eve exonerated

Not only does the Quran exonerate Eve from eating first from the tree, it clearly states that Adam was the one who was first deceived by Satan.

> We said, "O Adam! This is indeed an enemy of yours and your mate's. So do not let him expel you from paradise, or you will be miserable. Indeed you will neither be hungry in it nor naked. Indeed you will neither be thirsty in it, nor suffer from the sun." Then Satan tempted him. He said, "O Adam! Shall I show you the tree of immortality, and an imperishable kingdom?" So they both ate of it, and their nakedness became evident to them, and they began to stitch over themselves with the leaves of paradise. Adam disobeyed his Lord, and went amiss. (Quran 20:117–121)

Contrary to the Biblical story of Genesis, the Quran makes it clear that Satan went to Adam to deceive him and, thus, Eve only ate from the tree after Adam fell victim to Satan who had committed the second sin ever against God—the sin of lying.

> Then Satan tempted them, to expose to them what was hidden from them of their nakedness, and he said, "Your Lord has only forbidden you from this tree lest you should become angels, or lest you become immortal." And he swore to them, "I am indeed your well-wisher." (Quran 7:20–21)

Adam and Eve move to Earth

Adam, and Eve by association, only ate from the tree after Satan swore to them that they would become angels if they would only eat from the forbidden tree. They had never experienced lying before so they were quick to believe Satan's lie—especially when he assured them they would become angels, which meant they would worship God perfectly. Adam and Eve thought they would please God by eating from the tree based on this misunderstanding. Following eating from the tree, Adam and Eve were remorseful for having been deceived by Satan. They both equally pleaded with God to pardon them for their error.

They said, "Our Lord, we have wronged ourselves! If You do not forgive us and have mercy upon us, we will surely be among the losers." He said, "Get down, being enemies of one another! On the earth shall be your abode and sustenance for a time." He said, "In it you will live, and in it you will die; and from it you will be raised [from the dead]." "O Children of Adam! We have certainly sent down to you garments to cover your nakedness, and for adornment. Yet the garment of Godwariness—that is the best." That is [one] of Allah's signs, so that they may take admonition. "O Children of Adam! Do not let Satan tempt you, like he expelled your parents from paradise, stripping them of their garments to expose to them their nakedness. Indeed he sees you—he and his hosts— whence you do not see them. We have indeed made the devils friends of those who have no faith." When they commit an indecency, they say, "We found our fathers practising it, and Allah has enjoined it upon us." Say, "Indeed Allah does not enjoin indecencies. Do you attribute to Allah what you do not know?" (Quran 7:23–28)

God told Adam and Eve that they have violated His command not to eat from the tree. It was now time for them to depart paradise to Earth, as was always planned for them. Adam and Eve's presence on Earth, along with their progeny, is not viewed as punishment for humanity as is understood by the Biblical story—rather Earth was the intended destination for them anyway. It is clear in the Quran that Adam and

Eve were created from Earth to have dominion over it. Their presence in paradise was exclusive to the two of them at that stage, but they were to inhabit Earth at some point. Their eating from the tree may have expedited their presence on Earth, but it did not cause it.

By extension, the act of eating from the tree was not a sin against God but a violation to the detriment of Adam and Eve, for it rendered the paradise in which they lived immediately after their creation uninhabitable for them. God ordered them to depart to Earth but only after He pardoned them. He then promised to send them and their progeny prophets with messages of guidance from Him. He further promised that he who abides by the tenants of those messages should have no fear.

Refutation of doctrine of original sin

It is notable from the last Quranic verse cited above that those who blame their inclination to sin on the acts of their ancestors are mistaken.

> When they commit an indecency, they say, "We found our fathers practising it, and Allah has enjoined it upon us." Say, "Indeed Allah does not enjoin indecencies. Do you attribute to Allah what you do not know?" (Quran 7:28)

This appears to be a direct refute to the doctrine of original sin that was developed by St. Augustine.

Chapter Two

•••••••••◆◆◆•••••••••

Angels Versus Jinn

The existence of a being that is bent on misguiding the righteous is a theme common to many faiths. Islam holds a unique perspective on the original role and nature of Satan. Unlike Christians, Muslims do not believe that Satan is a fallen angel. Instead, he is a creature that God created from fire among a species of creatures referred to in the Quran as jinn (Quran 18:50). Members of this species possess the capability to commit sin just as their human counterparts do. This is an important distinction as Islam rejects the idea that angels have the capability to sway from their designated path from God. Furthermore, the Quran states that angels are created solely from light, as opposed to clay like humans, or fire like jinn (Quran 7:12–18).

Nature of Angels

The Quran refers to angels as the direct servants of God. One of their primary purposes is to relay the message of God unto humankind. Their every action is completed to fulfill the will of God, and they do not possess the capability to deviate from this responsibility. They are, in fact, completely infallible and must remain so in order to be pure beings that are capable of relaying the righteous message. Thus, if angels had the ability to become fallen, and were therefore able to commit sin or deviate from their duty to God, the message they relay would also be imperfect.

Role of Angels

According to Muslims, the role of angels differs very little from the concept of these holy beings held by most Christian sects. Perhaps the primary distinction between the Islamic and Christian understanding of angels is the scale on which they operate within our daily lives. Muslims believe that every human has, among others, two angels that accompany them from the point of their conception to the point at which the soul exits the body (death). These two angels are responsible for recording the good and bad deeds that their respective host commits. However, it is not just simple legislation these angels record. They are responsible for registering how the sins or good deeds a person commits affect their persona, soul, and, to an extent, even their physical appearance.

It is, of course, ultimately the decision of God as to what the outcome of one's actions is to be; however, God employs His host of infallible angels to carry out His laws. It is accepted in Islam and Christianity that Archangel Gabriel is responsible for the delivery of God's messages to His messengers. There are numerous examples of this occurrence in the Holy Quran. Prophet Muhammad received the dictation of the Quran itself directly from Gabriel who was conveying the message directly from God.

The responsibilities of angels exceed relaying divine messages to God's chosen messengers and recording the actions and nature of humankind. Angels are, in fact, responsible for maintaining the perfect equilibrium of nature and all of God's divine laws. They are behind every drop of rain that falls from the clouds, every storm that brews above us, and even the micro ecological miracles of bacteria and germs. It must be noted that angels are not working autonomously. In fact, God wills their every action, and they do not even possess the capability to act on free will.

Many believe that the Holy Spirit is an angel. There are two prevailing views in Islam about the Holy Spirit. The first, and most common, is that it is Archangel Gabriel. Although this view is the traditional one, many believe that it is a unique creation by God that is different from and, perhaps, higher than angels are.

Angels have many other roles according to the teachings of Islam. There are guardian angels who protect us from daily mishaps, there are angels who protect us from the whispers of the devils, and there are angels who are charged with causing us to die. However, Muslims believe that angels do not perform evil acts when they bring us death or calamity since they are only performing tasks that are ordained by God.

Lucifer (Satan) Is a Jinn

The Islamic perspective on the fall of Satan centers on the creation of Adam. The Quran states that when God created Adam, He commanded all of His angels to submit to His new creation. Present with the angels, and commanded by God to prostrate himself to Adam, was Lucifer (Iblis). Lucifer is the name of a jinn whom God allowed to reside among the angels. The story is recounted in the Quran:

Certainly We created you, then We formed you, then We said to the angels, "Prostrate before Adam." So they [all] prostrated, but not Iblis: he was not among those who prostrated. Said He, "What prevented you from prostrating, when I commanded you?" "I am better than him," he said. "You created me from fire and You created him from clay." "Get down from it!" He said. "It is not for you to be arrogant therein. Begone! You are indeed among the degraded ones." He said, "Respite me till the day they will be resurrected." Said He, "You are indeed among the reprieved." "As You have consigned me to perversity," he said, "I will surely lie in wait for them on Your straight path. Then I will come at them from their front and from their rear, and from their right and their left, and You will not find most of them to be grateful." Said He, "Begone hence, blameful, banished! Whoever of them follows you, I will surely fill hell with you all." (Quran 7:11–18)

The Quran makes a clear distinction between Iblis and angels as Iblis boasts of his composition of fire and the Quran states on numerous occasions that angels are created of pure light. As stated above, the incident where Iblis refused to prostrate himself to Adam because Adam was created of clay and Iblis of fire is seen by Islam as the root of all feelings of supremacy and, hence, the cause of all evil.

Lucifer As Humankind's Enemy

Out of spite and quest for revenge, Lucifer swore to misguide humankind and lead them to hell. Lucifer uses his many followers among jinn and people, who may or may not be aware that they serve his cause, to misguide people. The Quran makes it clear that Lucifer (Satan) is humanity's number one enemy and that we must guard ourselves against him and his soldiers. Muslims believe that every human being is well-equipped to protect themselves against Satan and his army of jinn and people and that God gave us the willpower, wisdom, and ability to gain knowledge.

Muslims and Christians agree that angels are pure, friendly beings who intend well for humankind. They also agree that Satan is humankind's number one enemy. Satan is a despised character in both traditions. There is also consensus that, without careful attention to our actions, people can be utilized by the forces of evil to do harm to our species and to Earth, for which God made us responsible because He gave us dominion over all that is in it.

Chapter Three

········◆◆◆········

The Role of Prophets and Messengers in Islam

It is He who created for you all that is in the earth. (Quran 2:29)

God created Adam and Eve to dwell on Earth along with their descendants (the human race) and were given dominion over Earth and all that it contains. However, a condition was laid upon Adam and Eve, along with the rest of humanity, that they must exercise this authority in accordance with God's laws. If people adhere to the laws, peace and harmony will exist on Earth, and God will reward the law-abiding people with paradise in the hereafter. If people violate these laws, then chaos, bloodshed, and corruption will become prevalent, disrupting the system according to which His universe must run (Quran 2:29). Those who do such things will be punished with hellfire (Quran 2:39).

We said: Go forth from this (state) all; so surely there will come to you a guidance from Me, then whoever follows My guidance, no fear shall come upon them, nor shall they grieve. (Quran 2:38)

Knowing God's Laws

Nevertheless, in order for people to abide by God's laws, they must first know what they are, and they must avoid any misinterpretation and misapplication of these laws. If the expectation were to obey these laws without knowing what they were or without a guarantee they were being correctly interpreted, then this would be unjust—which is against the very nature of God.

The main premise behind the concept of prophecy in Islam is the justice of God. The creation is essentially divided into categories of choice. Creatures belonging to the first category do not have choice in anything that governs their lives or destinies. This would include all objects, plants, and animals. A tree has no choice where it grows or what kind of tree it is and when and how it will become no more. Therefore, it is said that a tree has no choice or control over its destiny.

People, on the other hand, are given control over choosing between right and wrong. Right is defined as that which God declares as His law. Because God is just, He sends messages to people outlining what His laws are and gives examples of how to apply them. These messages must not contain any errors and must be interpreted correctly. Otherwise, how could God fairly judge people if errors are contained in the messages or their interpretations?

"This indeed is my straight path, so follow it, and do not follow [other] ways, for they will separate you from His way. This is what He enjoins upon you so that you may be Godwary." (Quran 6:153)

There is certainly a good exemplar for you in Abraham and those who were with him. (Quran 60:4)

When the Son of Mary was cited as an example...(Quran 43:57)

Prophets and Messengers

Because God's messages cannot contain any errors, those who interpret them must have full knowledge of everything they contain, and they must possess perfect knowledge of how to interpret and apply these messages. However, since people, in general, lack that perfect knowledge, God must choose those who will deliver and interpret these messages. God does this by choosing certain individuals from among people to whom He gives perfect knowledge and whom He perfects in wisdom and conduct so that they live and interpret His messages to humanity without error. God communicates messages to those chosen individuals by sending infallible angels in order to ensure these people themselves have full knowledge and understanding of these messages and will apply them flawlessly.

These chosen people must be infallible. Further, since everything that people do in their exercise of dominion over Earth affects God's system, these chosen people must not err at all. In other words, the chosen people must be infallible as related to every action. The messages must be understood and made clear by these people. God's chosen people who receive direct communication through His angels are called prophets.

Some prophets spoke directly to God, as in the case of Moses, or received revelation delivered by angels, like Abraham, Jesus, and Muhammad. They are some of the known prophets according to Islamic belief. As a rule, those prophets who received scripture to deliver are called messengers. Prophets who came to re-establish the messages of previous messengers are not called messengers. There were 124,000 prophets, but only a handful of them were messengers as well—bringing scripture to people.

Recognizing Messengers by Miracles

History tells us that since the days Adam and Eve first walked the earth, many people falsely claimed to be messengers of God. To avoid following false messengers, God has provided, by way of His books, certain characteristics that define "a messenger of God." The most obvious and noteworthy of these characteristics is the ability to perform miracles from God. Miracles cannot be duplicated and challenge a prevalent issue facing the people at the time. A messenger has the ability to deliver and interpret the message of the miracle.

An example of such a miracle occurred during the time of Moses. Magic was a dominant issue during Moses' time. God gave Moses the power to turn his staff into a real snake that engulfed the staffs of the magicians. The message of that particular miracle was to prove the point that God is more powerful than the magic that a person can create.

Another, perhaps more famous, miracle of Moses is the account of the Red Sea. When the Children of Israel were fleeing the wrath of the pharaoh of the time, Moses parted the Red Sea and led them in their escape.

At the time that Jesus was sent to the Children of Israel, diseases were rampant. Medicine men were considered to be among the most elite. God gave Jesus the power to cure any disease and to bring back to life those who perished because of those diseases.

During the sixth century, people were ruled by the beauty of poetry and the mastery of language. These people were also worshipping idols they believed controlled the universe. Therefore, God gave Muhammad the Quran. Muslim scholars point out the miraculous language of the Quran in Arabic. Prophet Muhammad also performed other miracles relevant to his time and place.

Muhammad once asked the Meccans if he could bring them a sign that would convince them he was a messenger. The Meccans challenged him to have a tree come to him and said that if he did they would believe in his message. When Prophet Muhammad ordered the tree to come to him, it did and then bowed to him. Some of the Meccans believed Muhammad while others claimed he had performed magic on the tree.

Messengers Bring Consistent Scripture

Though miracles play a large role in addressing a present need of the time, God has provided additional proof to validate an individual as a messenger. Each messenger must deliver a consistent message of obedience to God's law. If the messengers delivered messages that differed from one another, then one could conclude the source of the messages was not the same. However, since the messages all came from the one God, they must contain the same spirit of law. Although further elaboration or application of the law may change from one era to another, as in specific cases that apply to certain times or cultures, the overall teachings of God's laws are the same. It is for this reason that all divine religions teach the importance of the Ten Commandments and other canons.

Muslims believe that the differences which came to exist between Judaism, Christianity, and Islam were caused by intentional and unintentional changes in the original messages delivered by Moses and Jesus.

Muslims must equally believe in all of God's messages and revere all of His prophets without distinction. The Holy Quran states:

Say, "We have faith in Allah, and that which has been sent down to us, and that which was sent down to Abraham, Ishmael, Isaac, Jacob and the Tribes, and that which Moses and Jesus were given, and that which the prophets were given from their Lord; we make no distinction between any of them, and to Him do we submit." (Quran 2:136)

Chapter Four

························◆◆◆◆·······

The Relationship Between Christianity and Islam

Prophet Muhammad Fulfilled Prophecy

Learned believers at the time of Prophet Muhammad were expecting the promised prophet to be raised in Arabia. The Christian monk Baheirah recognized 12-year old Muhammad as "the prophet foretold in the scriptures." When Waraqah ibn Nawfal, whom we shall discuss later, immediately acknowledged Muhammad to be the awaited prophet, many Christians of the time became Muslims.

Jesus Revered in Islam

Islam gives Jesus (peace be upon him) a lofty place in God's creation but as a prophet, not as God. Muslims believe that Jesus was indeed miraculously born to a virgin mother, without a father, and that he is the promised Messiah whom God promised the Jews and the rest of the world.

In fact, the Muslim belief that Jesus is God's promised Messiah is the central issue of disagreement between Jews and Muslims. According to Islam, God promised the Jews the Holy Land, provided they believe in Jesus as the Messiah. In other words, Muslims contend that God's covenant with the Jews was a conditional one. Jews must accept Jesus as the Messiah, otherwise, they would not qualify to gain possession of the Holy Land. From the view of Muslims, since Jews do not accept Jesus as the promised Messiah, they broke God's covenant and are no longer qualified to possess the Holy Land.

Muslims and Christians agree that Jesus rose to heaven to be seated next to the throne of God, although Muslims do not believe that Jesus died before he ascended. They both hold fast the belief that God sent down the Holy Spirit to be with Jesus while on Earth.

The Quran also teaches that Jesus performed amazing miracles, such as curing the ill, walking on water, and raising the dead, but Islam teaches that he performed miracles by God's will . . . like other prophets did—not because he was God.

And [he will be] an apostle to the Children of Israel, [and he will declare,] "I have certainly brought you a sign from your Lord: I will create for you out of clay the form of a bird, then I will breathe into it, and it will become a bird by Allah's leave. And I heal the blind and the leper and I revive the dead by Allah's leave. And I will tell you what you have eaten and what you have stored in your houses. There is indeed a sign in that for you, should you be faithful." (Quran 3:49)

The Virgin Mary and Jesus Mentioned in the Quran

A complete chapter of the Quran is named "The Virgin Mary" and accounts the story of Jesus Christ's infancy.

In the name of God, the Most Compassionate, the Most Merciful

Kaf, Ha, Ya, ʿAyn, Sad. [This is] an account of your Lord's mercy on His servant, Zechariah, when he called out to his Lord with a secret cry. He said, "My Lord! Indeed my bones have become feeble, and my head has turned white with age, yet never have I, my Lord, been disappointed in supplicating You! Indeed I fear my kinsmen, after me, and my wife is barren. So grant me from Yourself an heir who may inherit from me and inherit from the House of Jacob, and make him, my Lord, pleasing [to You]!"

"O Zechariah! Indeed We give you the good news of a son, whose name is 'John.' Never before have We made anyone his namesake." He said, "My Lord! How shall I have a son, when my wife is barren, and I am already advanced in age?" He said, "So shall it be. Your Lord has said, 'It is simple for Me.' Certainly I created you before when you were nothing." He said, "My Lord! Appoint a sign for me." He said, "Your sign is that you will not speak to the people for three complete nights." So he emerged before his people from the Temple, and signaled to them that they should glorify [Allah] morning and evening.

"O John!" [We said,] "Hold on with power to the Book!" And We gave him judgement while still a child, and a compassion and purity from Us. He was Godwary, and good to his parents, and was not self-willed or disobedient. Peace be to him, the day he was born, and the day he dies, and the day he is raised alive!

And mention in the Book Mary, when she withdrew from her family to an easterly place. Thus did she seclude herself from them, whereupon We sent to her Our Spirit and he became incarnate for her as a well-proportioned human. She said, "I seek the protection of the All-beneficent from you, should you be Godwary!" He said, "I am only a messenger of your Lord that I may give you a pure son." She said, "How shall I have a child seeing that no human being has ever touched

27

me, nor have I been unchaste?" He said, "So shall it be. Your Lord says, "It is simple for Me." And so that We may make him a sign for mankind and a mercy from Us, and it is a matter [already] decided."

Thus she conceived him, then withdrew with him to a distant place. The birth pangs brought her to the trunk of a date palm. She said, "I wish I had died before this and become a forgotten thing, beyond recall." Thereupon he called her from below her [saying,] "Do not grieve! Your Lord has made a spring to flow at your feet. Shake the trunk of the palm tree, freshly picked dates will drop upon you. Eat, drink, and be comforted. Then if you see any human, say, 'Indeed I have vowed a fast to the All-beneficent, so I will not speak to any human today.'"

Then carrying him she brought him to her people. They said, "O Mary, you have certainly come up with an odd thing! O sister of Aaron['s lineage]! Your father was not an evil man, nor was your mother unchaste." Thereat she pointed to him. They said, "How can we speak to one who is yet a baby in the cradle?" He said, "Indeed I am a servant of Allah! He has given me the Book and made me a prophet. He has made me blessed, wherever I may be, and He has enjoined me to [maintain] the prayer and to [pay] the zakat as long as I live, and to be good to my mother, and He has not made me self-willed and wretched. Peace is to me the day I was born, and the day I die, and the day I am raised alive."

That is Jesus, son of Mary, a Word of the Real concerning whom they are in doubt. It is not for Allah to take a son. Immaculate is He! When He decides on a matter, He just says to it, "Be!" and it is. "Indeed Allah is my Lord and your Lord. So worship Him. This is a straight path." (Quran 19:1–36)

It's known to Shia Muslims that Mary was present at the birth of Prophet Muhammad's daughter Fatima—not in her earthly body, we assume, for she would have been passed away by then. When it came time for Prophet Muhammad's wife Khadija to give birth, she sent for midwives from among her people (Quraysh), but none would help her saying, "We will not help you; for you became Muhammad's wife. The story continues:

During childbirth, four ladies whose beauty and brilliance were indescribable entered the house. One of them said, "I am your mother, Eve." The second said, "I am Umm Kulthum, Moses' sister." The third said, "I am Mary, and we have come to help you."[10]

Christian-Muslim Cooperation

The histories of Islam and Christianity are intertwined in many ways—more than is apparent to the layperson. For example, most Christians are not aware of the role Christianity played in the birth of Islam. Early Christian support for and the protection of Muslims by a Christian leader helped Islam survive an existential threat by the Meccans.

A just Christian king protects early Muslims

Prophet Muhammad ordered a large group of his followers to escape persecution by taking refuge in Abyssinia, where a "just Christian king" would afford them protection. Indeed, King Nagos[11] refused to hand over the early Muslims to the polytheist Meccans because he viewed the difference between Islam and Christianity as "thinner than the

---

10. Abu Muhammad Ordoni, *Fatima the Gracious*, (Qum: Ansariyan Publications), accessed 2016, http://www.al-islam.org/fatima-the-gracious-abu-muhammad-ordoni.
11. *Najashi* in Arabic

line drawn in the sand." It is reported that the Prophet was deeply saddened when he heard of the demise of his friend, King Nagos, and led a special prayer service for his Christian friend. Years later, the Muslim refugees he had protected returned to Medina where Islam established its first capital.

Christians allowed to use a mosque for worship

When Islam was strengthened in the city of Medina and the Prophet was able to engage other groups in debate and discussions, he invited the Christians of Najran, a province in Arabia, to debate the similarities and differences between the two faiths. Upon their arrival, Prophet Muhammad ordered his mosque, the second holiest of all places in Islam, to be emptied to make way for the Christian guests to hold their prayer services without interference. The Christians then "set up their mass, rang their bells, and erected their crosses."[12]

Christians come to the aid of the Prophet's grandson

At a time when government forces besieged the Prophet's grandson, Hussain (peace be upon him), devout Christian friends sided with him and, in fact, died defending his cause of standing against oppression. Nowadays, Christians join Shia Muslims in modern-day Karbala, Iraq to commemorate those deaths. The commemoration is a "universal, borderless, and meta-religious symbol of freedom and compassion."[13]

---

12. Sayid Jaffer Murtadha al-Amuli, *Concise History of the Magnificent Prophet Muhammad,* vol 1, p. 155.
13. Sayed Mahdi al-Modarresi, "World's Biggest Pilgrimage Now Underway, And Why You've Never Heard of it!" The Huffington Post, November 24, 2014, accessed January 2016, http://www.huffingtonpost.co.uk/sayed-mahdi-almodarresi/arbaeen-pilgrimage_b_6203756.html.

Coptic Christians help

Although many in current day Western Christendom have painted an image of historical confrontation between Islam and Christianity, history shows the reality to be quite to the contrary.

When the Muslim conquests started after the death of Prophet Muhammad, the Muslim military leader of Egypt, Amr ibn al-As, sought and secured the help of Coptic Christians who were willing participants in the Muslim quest to root out Byzantine armies from Egypt. When al-As desired to continue his quests further west, he asked Pope Benyamin (Benjamin) of the Coptic Church to hold a service at the largest Christian church to pray for victory of the Muslim armies. Not only did the Pope oblige, but he also escorted the Muslim army to the limits of the city of Alexandria in a clear show of support.

It is important to point out that Shia Islam doesn't agree with those conquests and considers them to be in clear violation of the teachings of the Quran. Furthermore, Shia Muslims hold a negative view of the leaders of those conquests.

Christians Mentioned in the Quran

Acts of solidarity between early Muslims and Christians were consistent with the kind and loving way the Quran refers to Christians. For example, the Quran says about Christians:

And We followed them with Jesus son of Mary, to confirm that which was before him of the Torah, and We gave him the Evangel containing guidance and light, confirming what was before it of the Torah, and as guidance and advice for the Godwary. (Quran 5:46)

And surely you will find the nearest of them in affection to the faithful to be those who say "We are Christians." That is because there are priests and monks among them, and because they are not arrogant. When they hear what has been revealed to the Apostle, you see their eyes fill with tears because of the truth that they recognize. They say, "Our Lord, we believe; so write us down among the witnesses. Why should we not believe in Allah and the truth that has come to us, eager as we are that our Lord should admit us among the righteous people?" So, for what they said, Allah requited them with gardens with streams running in them, to remain in them [forever], and that is the reward of the virtuous. (Quran 5:82–85)

Conclusion

Islam and Christianity share the belief in Jesus as the only promised Messiah, born of the Virgin Mary, by way of a unique miracle, unparalleled in human history. Both faiths posit that Jesus Christ will return to establish the kingdom of God. Churches and mosques alike display the name of God, *Allah*, in a show of absolute devotion to the one Almighty God. Both consider the period of the Old Testament to be the beginning of their story. Both consider the Ten Commandments to be foundational to their moral code, and they share the same high moral integrity based on teachings that are central to their faiths. Despite this, the shared consciousness of the followers of Christianity and Islam has been shaped to place the two faiths at odds.

Chapter Five

How Christianity and Islam Differ

There remain differences in the respective belief systems that are foundational to Christianity and Islam. Central to those differences are two topics: the doctrine of the trinity within Christianity, which Islam rejects outright, and Islam's teaching that Jesus didn't die on the cross but was instead raised to heaven while still alive.

Upon careful examination, Islam can truly be viewed as a corrective movement to Christianity. We shall examine each point separately arguing that Christians should accept Islam as a faith prophesied by Jesus himself, preceded by other prophets such as Moses and Isaiah, among others (peace be upon them all).

Challenges to the Trinity

Although Muslims accept Christians as brothers in faith, they also take issue with the doctrine of the trinity. Muslims believe that Jesus Christ was a servant of God's cause and a prophet, but not God, or a part of God.

Scripture says Jesus is not God

The Quran tells us that Jesus would not be too proud to be a servant of His cause and clearly submits himself to God. The trinity and divinity of Jesus are clearly contended in the Quran. In the Quranic chapter, Women (*al-Nisa*), God speaks directly to Christians:

O People of the Book! Do not exceed the bounds in your religion, and do not attribute anything to Allah except the truth. The Messiah, Jesus son of Mary, was only an apostle of Allah, and His Word that He cast toward Mary and a spirit from Him. So have faith in Allah and His apostles, and do not say, "[God is] a trinity." Relinquish [such a creed]! That is better for you. Allah is but the One God. He is far too immaculate to have any son. To Him belongs whatever is in the heavens and whatever is on the earth, and Allah suffices as trustee.

The Messiah would never disdain being a servant of Allah, nor would the angels brought near [to Him]. And whoever disdains His worship and is arrogant, He will gather them all toward Him. (Quran 4:171–172)

As prophesied in the Quran and the Bible, Jesus will deny having told his followers to worship him. The Prophet Jesus denies anything to do with the invention of the trinity or the divinity of himself or his mother.

And when Allah will say, "O Jesus son of Mary! Was it you who said to the people, 'Take me and my mother for gods besides Allah'?" He will say, "Immaculate are You! It does not behoove me to say what I have no right to [say]. Had I said it, You would certainly have known it: You know whatever is in my self, and I do not know what is in Your Self. Indeed You are knower of all that is Unseen.

I did not say to them [anything] except what You had commanded me [to say]: 'Worship Allah, my Lord and your Lord.' And I was a witness to them so long as I was among them. But when You had taken me away, You Yourself were

watchful over them, and You are witness to all things."
(Quran 5:116–17)

And in the New Testament, in Mark, Jesus speaks of God as not being himself (Jesus):

Now as He was going out on the road, one came running, knelt before Him, and asked Him, "Good Teacher, what shall I do that I may inherit eternal life?" So Jesus said to him, "Why do you call Me Good? No one is Good but One that is, God. You know the commandments: 'Do not commit adultery,' 'Do not murder,' 'Do not steal,' 'Do not bear false witness,' 'Do not defraud,' 'Honor your father and your mother.'" (Mark 10:17–22)

Based on these and other verses from the Quran (e.g., 5:72–74) and Bible in which Jesus places himself at a degree of subservience to God, Muslims argue the invalidity of the trinity and refute high Christology verses, often used by Trinitarian Christians. Islam, as a faith, rejects the idea that Jesus Christ is equal to God and attributes those verses to inconsistencies in translation and man-made concepts that made their way into Christianity after Jesus' departure.

Perhaps high Christology made its way into the faith because of the belief shared by both Muslims and Christians about the miraculous birth of Jesus. However, God reminds us in the Quran that this miracle is no more a miracle than the creation of Adam with no father or mother.

Indeed the case of Jesus with Allah is like the case of Adam: He created him from dust, then said to him, "Be," and he was. (Quran 3:59)

God is one

Jesus kept reminding the Jews and his followers of the first and most important commandment, pointing out that God has no equal associate. In Mark, Jesus answered him, "The first of all the commandments is: 'Hear, O Israel, the LORD our God, the LORD is one'" (Mark 12:29). This verse, quoting Deuteronomy 6:4, confirms God's oneness: "Hear, O Israel: The LORD our God, the LORD is one!"

Perhaps the most telling verse that clearly supports the Muslim view that Jesus is God's chosen messenger is apparent when John states, "And this is eternal life, that they may know You, the only true God, and Jesus Christ whom You have sent" (John 17:3). These verses, Muslims argue, are consistent with the teachings of the Old Testament and the Quran. For example, in Deuteronomy it says, "Therefore know this day, and consider it in your heart, that the LORD Himself is God in heaven above and on the earth beneath; there is no other" (Deuteronomy 4:39).

This monotheistic theme is maintained throughout the Old Testament and by later prophets. Isaiah references this fact in many places:

Thus says the LORD, the King of Israel,
And his Redeemer, the LORD of hosts:
"I am the First and I am the Last;
Besides Me there is no God." (Isaiah 44:6)

"I am the LORD, and there is no other;
There is no God besides Me.
I will gird you, though you have not known Me,
That they may know from the rising of the sun to its setting
That there is none besides Me.
I am the LORD, and there is no other;
I form the light and create darkness,
I make peace and create calamity;
I, the LORD, do all these things." (Isaiah 45:5–7)

Remember the former things of old,
For I am God, and there is no other;
I am God, and there is none like Me. (Isaiah 46:9)

Despite the aforementioned verses that clearly support pure monotheism, which Islam advocates, development of the trinity within Christianity cannot be understood without a review of the historical context in which it developed.

Early Christians rejected the trinity

Since Jesus stated in the Sermon on the Mount that he did not come to change the law, it follows that the most fundamental teaching of Judaism (i.e., pure monotheism) must be preserved in his teachings. This fact can be seen in the teachings of early Christians. In fact, it is evident from the writings of the early adopters of the trinity that the majority of Christians rejected this new doctrine and found it to be in violation of their "Rule of Faith." Tertullian gave us a glimpse into the intense challenge which Christianity, and by extension the Roman Empire, faced in attempting to affect a drastic change from the then-popular polytheistic beliefs of the majority of Romans, who were not Christians, to that of believing in one God (as believed by the majority of Christians). Tertullian wrote:

The simple, indeed (I will not call them unwise or unlearned), who always constitute the majority of believers, are startled at the dispensation (of the Three in One), on the very ground that their very Rule of Faith withdraws them from the world's plurality of gods to the one only true God; not understanding that, although He is the one only God, He must yet be believed in with His own economy.[14]

---

14. Tertullian, *Against Praxeas,* (Grand Rapids: Eerdmans, 1977).

That which caused the Christian establishment to depart from the most fundamental teaching of all previous prophets before Jesus (and revert to the insertion of a complex form of Godhead) can be understood if one takes a closer look at the societal composition of the Roman Empire at the time.

Compromising the faith for the sake of conversions

It is well established that Paul had to depart from key Jewish teachings, such as circumcision and the prohibition of consuming swine flesh, to accommodate the otherwise resistant pagans of the areas north of Palestine. These two examples are clear indications of a change, which according to Paul, was a prerequisite to invite people to the new Christian faith, despite strong opposition by Simon Peter and the Jerusalem Church. Christians who followed Simon Peter continued to follow Mosaic law, which Jesus declared he would not change, which included not consuming swine flesh and being circumcised.

Although in clear violation of Mosaic law, Paul's success in legitimizing these changes paved the way for more profound changes later on. The changes that were in concurrence with Paul's view would challenge the most fundamental Judeo-Christian teachings of pure and simple monotheism.

The Roman Empire was faced with a socio-religious challenge that threatened its national security. The vast majority of the empire's inhabitants practiced and believed in a slew of pagan religions. Yet the new Christians, who were increasing in number and having great success at converting many communities, including many intellectuals, rejected those forms of polytheistic beliefs. This created a situation that could have led to a disastrous internal religious strife with the potential to dismantle the otherwise strong empire from within.

Under this backdrop, Christian intellectuals, motivated by strengthening the empire in order to stabilize it and further accommodate its pagan population, started debating various forms of pagan ideologies surrounding the nature of God. The most prevalent ideology was that of a trinity shrouded in a "mysterious" Godhead.

Paul, who introduced the idea of religious modification for the sake of conversion, started speaking of what could be seen as an early form of a trinity. It is notable that Paul himself referred to the nature of God as a mystery:

> A good case can be made that Paul presented the Gospel to Gentiles in such a way that the non-Jews within the Roman Empire would be converted. Gentiles would not be interested in a Jewish Messiah and the law given by Moses, but might be interested in a "Christ" that in some ways resembled other historical and mythological figures known from various mystery religions whose adherents lived within the Roman Empire.[15]

Jesus didn't teach the trinity

Jesus himself never advocated the trinity. It violates the very fundamental basis of his teachings, the belief in one God. Jesus clearly states so in yet another passage of the Bible (Matthew 20:23) when he said, "'You will drink my cup, but to sit at my right hand and at my left is not mine to grant, but it is for those for whom it has been prepared by my Father.'"

Philip Voerding, in his book *The Trouble with Christianity*, makes the following conclusion regarding the above-mentioned passage:

> Jesus is stating that, contrary to the Western view of the Trinity doctrine that the Son is co-equal with the Father, this

15. Philip Voerding, *The Trouble with Christianity*, (AuthorHouse: 2009.)

is indeed not so. In fact, we would expect the One True God, by definition, to be able to do anything within His perfect moral character. Since Jesus states he cannot do something that the Father can do, not only is the "the son" not coequal with the Father, but "the son" cannot be eternal God, otherwise he would have the right to fulfill this request.[16]

▲

Jesus Wasn't Crucified

Trinitarian Christians submit to the story of Jesus' crucifixion as a historical fact and base many of their foundational beliefs on this submission. Muslims, on the other hand, dispute this submission and argue that Jesus was not crucified. They base their arguments on a number of issues including theology, Biblical clarity, and historical fact.

However, the issue of whether Jesus would die for his faith is not in question for Muslims, and, indeed, Christians believe that martyrdom is a praiseworthy act when called for. Both Islam and Christianity gave many martyrs over time to protect their faiths. Christians, in fact, gave many more martyrs to protect their faith than Muslims as the total number of people who died fighting against and for Islam leading up to the death of Prophet Muhammad did not exceed 600. Since Muslims won the majority of those existential battles against the enemies of the faith, it is noted that the majority of those killed in Islam's early wars were not Muslims. Therefore, the number of Muslims who died defending the faith does not exceed several hundred.

On the other hand, Christians were fiercely fought and persecuted by their early enemies, and many more of them were tortured and killed, forcing them to flee Palestine to the surrounding areas including Jordan where the oldest Christian churches are found, many in underground caves. Paul, who later became a central figure to

---

16. Ibid.

Trinitarian Christianity, was a leading figure in torturing and killing the Christian faithful early on.

Jesus' mission incomplete

Muslims believe in Jesus as the promised Messiah whose role, as the only promised and true Messiah, is to establish God's kingdom on Earth. Thus, Muslims argue that to accept the story of the crucifixion of Jesus as understood by Trinitarian Christians would violate the very meaning of Jesus being the Messiah. To state that God allowed the murder of Jesus before he fulfilled his role as the Messiah, which is to establish the kingdom of God, would violate his role as the promised Messiah. Instead, Muslims contend, God protected Jesus by raising him up to heaven where he is seated next to the throne of God, waiting until his time to return and fulfill his task as the Messiah. A Shia Muslim narration says, "Jesus the son of Mary is the Spirit of Allah and His Word. He was thirty-three years old in the world. Then Allah raised him to heaven. He will descend to the earth and it is he who will kill the Antichrist (*Dajjal*)."[17]

Jesus was not able to complete his task the first time around because humanity was simply not ready to receive all that he had to teach. The wisdom of his first coming is clear in that it was the first phase in preparing humanity for the end of times. In other words, his first coming was not a failure but a prerequisite to his final and more important coming.

As we shall explain below, Muslims argue that Jesus prophesied the coming of Prophet Muhammad, who in Jesus' words, would communicate all of God's words to humanity, as humanity was not

---

17. Mahdi Muntazir Qaim, *Jesus through Shiite Narrations,* (Qum: Ansariyan Publications), accessed January 2016, http://www.al-islam.org/jesus-though-shiite-narrations-mahdi-muntazir-qaim.

yet ready for what he (Jesus) had to say. Jesus clearly stated so in the following verse:

> I have yet many things to say unto you, but ye cannot bear them now. Howbeit when he, the Spirit of truth is come, he will guide you unto all truth: for he shall not speak of himself; but whatsoever he shall hear, that shall he speak: and he will show you things to come. He shall glorify me. (John 16:12–14)

God's compassion

Furthermore, one of God's named traits (according to the Islamic belief in God's ninety-nine names) is that He is merciful and compassionate. Both Muslims and Christians accept the story of Abraham's willingness to sacrifice his son to please God. They also accept the fact that God, by His mercy and compassion, saved Abraham's son by sending down a ram to be slaughtered instead. So Muslims ask: If Jesus was God's begotten son, as Trinitarian Christians contest, then wouldn't He be more merciful and compassionate with His own son than with the son of His servant, Abraham? In other words, God's ultimate love for Jesus would not have permitted the murder of the Christ.

No need for atonement

There are numerous additional theological arguments brought by Muslims to refute the story of crucifixion that are outside of the scope of this work. Trinitarian Christians have also developed a number of arguments to justify Jesus' crucifixion, one of which is that "he died for our sins" as originated by Paul, although not entirely formulated by him, and that God must be paid back for the violation which took place during the story of creation—an argument known by some as the satisfaction theory of the atonement—God sacrificed Jesus to be paid back.

Muslims subscribe to neither argument. The first, in Muslims' view, violates God's ultimate mercy and compassion. Since God is the most merciful, He has the power to forgive all sins without the shedding of anyone's blood, especially that of Jesus Christ. Further, to state that God has to be paid back is to state that He is not all-powerful and is need of retribution, which would make Him less than God. Who, after all, forces God to be bound by any law, and one where He can only be paid back by the murder of His own son, as some Christians contend, except a being more powerful than God himself? This being does not exist according to both Muslim and Christian teachings.

Both Muslims and Christians agree that Jesus did not come to change the fundamental teachings of Moses, although he did indeed eliminate the need for blood sacrifice for the forgiveness of sins according to both Muslims and Christians (and he permitted the consumption of pork according to Christians who follow Paul). If this is the case, Muslims ask, why would Jesus have to be sacrificed for the atonement of sins if God no longer required blood sacrifice for the same thing?

Biblical narrative is unclear

People didn't know how Jesus looked

Muslims argue that the Bible itself does not conclusively support the view that Jesus was crucified. It is evident from the Biblical narratives that, although Jesus was known by name and character, many people, including the Sanhedrin and Roman soldiers, did not physically know him. This is evidenced by the fact that Judas had to be hired as a spy and eyewitness to identify Jesus so that he could be captured:

43 And immediately, while he yet spoke, cometh Judas, one of the twelve, and with him a great multitude with swords and staves, from the chief priests and the scribes and the elders.

44 And he that betrayed him had given them a token, saying, Whomsoever I shall kiss, that same is he; take him, and lead him away safely.

45 And as soon as he was come, he goeth straightway to him, and saith, Master, master; and kissed him.

46 And they laid their hands on him, and took him.

47 And one of them that stood by drew a sword, and smote a servant of the high priest, and cut off his ear.

48 And Jesus answered and said unto them, Are ye come out, as against a thief, with swords and with staves to take me?

49 I was daily with you in the temple teaching, and ye took me not: but the scriptures must be fulfilled.

50 And they all forsook him, and fled.

51 And there followed him a certain young man, having a linen cloth cast about his naked body; and the young men laid hold on him:

52 And he left the linen cloth, and fled from them naked.

53 And they led Jesus away to the high priest: and with him were assembled all the chief priests and the elders and the scribes.

54 And Peter followed him afar off, even into the palace of the high priest: and he sat with the servants, and warmed himself at the fire.

55 And the chief priests and all the council sought for witness against Jesus to put him to death; and found none. (Mark 14)

Furthermore, the disciples, the only reliable witnesses who could positively identify Jesus, fled upon his capture. The only one who did not flee, Peter, followed him from afar, and even he denied that the captured person was Jesus, cursing him to prove the point. The authorities' repeated attempts to locate individuals who could positively identify Jesus by person are further evidence that Jesus was not familiar in person to many people. This is due to the fact that pictures and other forms of identification were not available during that time.

Simon of Cyrene bore the cross

Moreover, when Jesus was no longer able to continue to carry the cross after being repeatedly tortured, the cross was taken away from his back and placed on the back of Simon of Cyrene. Nowhere does the Bible tell us that the cross was placed again on the back of Jesus, casting further doubt that the man on the cross was indeed the Messiah:

---

27 Then the soldiers of the governor took Jesus into the common hall, and gathered unto him the whole band of soldiers.

28 And they stripped him, and put on him a scarlet robe.

29 And when they had platted a crown of thorns, they put it upon his head, and a reed in his right hand: and they bowed the knee before him, and mocked him, saying, Hail, King of the Jews!

30 And they spit upon him, and took the reed, and smote him on the head.

31 And after that they had mocked him, they took the robe off from him, and put his own raiment on him, and led him away to crucify him.

32 And as they came out, they found a man of Cyrene, Simon by name: him they compelled to bear his cross.

33 And when they were come unto a place called Golgotha, that is to say, a place of a skull,

34 They gave him vinegar to drink mingled with gall: and when he had tasted thereof, he would not drink.

35 And they crucified him, and parted his garments, casting lots: that it might be fulfilled which was spoken by the prophet, They parted my garments among them, and upon my vesture did they cast lots.

36 And sitting down they watched him there. (Matthew 27)

Jesus' behavior on the cross

This doubt is exacerbated by the contrary character and behavior of the man on the cross to that of Jesus. The Gospels tell of the cries of the man on the cross in objection to his plight as he was crying:

Now from the sixth hour darkness fell upon all the land until the ninth hour. And about the ninth hour Jesus cried out with a loud voice, saying, "Eli, Eli, lama sabachthani?" that is, "My God, My God, why hast Thou forsaken Me?" (Matthew 27:45–46)

Why, if this was indeed Jesus on the cross, would he believe that his Lord had forsaken him when the Bible tells us that just a short time before, Jesus submitted to his possible fate:

And He went a little beyond them, and fell on His face and prayed, saying, "My Father, if it is possible, let this cup pass from Me; yet not as I will, but as You will." (Matthew 26:39)

If Jesus knew that he would be seated next to God in three days and that his death would atone for the sins of humankind, why would he object to it in this fashion?

A common Christian answer to these questions is that Jesus was repeating a prayer from the Psalm 22:1. Yet, the questions persist. Why would Jesus react in this fashion to an otherwise great sacrifice? Christianity gave many a martyr. According to Tertullian, "The blood of the martyrs is the seed of the Church." Truly, the most famous statement is that of Ignatius, the Martyr of Antioch,[18] who is said to have known the Apostle John, who accordingly lived to an old age but suffered imprisonment and torture:

I am writing to all the Churches and I enjoin all that I am dying willingly for God's sake, if only you do not prevent it. I beg you, do not do me an untimely kindness. Allow me to be eaten by the beasts, which are my way of reaching to God. I am God's wheat, and I am to be ground by the teeth of wild beasts, so that I may become the pure bread of Christ.[19]

Could these martyrs have been greater in their faith and sacrifice than the patriarch of the faith himself, Jesus Christ? Muslims say no, since the man on the cross was not Jesus.

Mary's demeanor

Mary's observance of the crucifixion, and the man's cries, did not reflect that of a mother who was witnessing her son experiencing such pain and suffering. Yes, her mood was somber as the mood of any human witnessing the death of another, even a criminal, but it certainly was not the mood of an average mother, or the mother of the Messiah Jesus Christ.

---

18. circa 120 CE
19. Letter to the Romans

Jesus trying to prove he was not a ghost

Muslims further contend that Jesus himself denied that he was crucified when he tried to prove to the disciples that he was not a ghost. When Jesus appeared to the disciples three days after the cross was erected, Jesus scolded his disciples because they reacted as if they have seen a ghost. To prove that he was alive, Jesus asked them for bread and fish of which he ate and made them feel his torture wounds. However, Jesus taught his followers that death turns one into a ghost with no physical needs, as ghosts are only spirits.

In the Gospel of Luke, Jesus refutes the Pharisees' question by explaining that upon their deaths, the woman in question and her seven husbands will be ghosts, and thus have no physical needs.

---

28 Saying, Master, Moses wrote unto us, If any man's brother die, having a wife, and he die without children, that his brother should take his wife, and raise up seed unto his brother.

29 There were therefore seven brethren: and the first took a wife, and died without children.

30 And the second took her to wife, and he died childless.

31 And the third took her; and in like manner the seven also: and they left no children, and died.

32 Last of all the woman died also.

33 Therefore in the resurrection whose wife of them is she? For seven had her to wife.

34 And Jesus answering said unto them, The children of this world marry, and are given in marriage:

35 But they which shall be accounted worthy to obtain that world, and the resurrection from the dead, neither marry, nor are given in marriage:

36 Neither can they die any more: for they are equal unto the
angels; and are the children of God, being the children of
the resurrection. (Luke 20)

Thus, if Jesus did indeed die on the cross, then he would have come back
as a ghost. He would not have scolded his disciples for their reactions,
nor tried to ask for bread and fish to prove that he was not a ghost.

Conclusion

These points which Muslims raise are further strengthened by several
other Biblical statements and inconsistencies, such as the fact the
Bible itself does not agree on which day the crucifixion took place or
Pilate's wife's attempt to persuade her husband not to crucify Jesus
and he "washed his hands" of the death of Jesus—in addition to his
attempt to persuade the Sanhedrin to kill another man in place of Jesus.

In short, Muslims believe that since Jesus is the only promised Messiah
whose task is to establish the Kingdom of God on Earth, God did not
permit his killing but instead raised him up to heaven where he is
seated next to His throne until God sends him back to fulfill his task.
Muslims support their belief using several other arguments, including
arguments derived from Biblical texts, as we have pointed out above.

Chapter Six

·············◆·◈·◆·············

Biblical Prophecies Foretell the Coming of Islam and Prophet Muhammad

In anticipation of the coming of the promised prophet as foretold in both the Old and New Testaments, Jewish and Christian groups and individuals started to turn their attention to Mecca and Yathrib. Approximately 200 years before the coming of Prophet Muhammad, two Jewish tribes emigrated from Palestine and settled in Yathrib, which was later renamed Medina by Prophet Muhammad. Another Arab tribe converted to Judaism and moved to Medina to join their Jewish brethren in anticipation of the promised prophet. The Jews of Medina drew strength from their scriptures, foretelling the coming of the new prophet. They used to threaten the non-Jewish citizens of Medina that when the new prophet comes, he will lead the Jews in victory over non-Jews. In fact, the Quran laid blame on the Jews of Medina for not rallying behind the Prophet after he came.

Christians, on the other hand, focused their attention on Mecca. Successive delegations visited Mecca to investigate signs indicating the close advent of the prophet. One notable Christian, a man by the name of Waraqah ibn Nawfal, decided to relocate to Mecca to wait for the new prophet. The name *Waraqah* means "the scroll"—a possible indication that he was well-learned. Muslims agree that Waraqah accepted Muhammad as the promised prophet on the very first day the Prophet descended from the mountain after having received the first revelation.

The City of Mecca and the Well of Zamzam

Jews and Christians found many references in their scriptures to this new prophet. One verse we know of today clearly states the Prophet by name while others prophesied the city where he and his followers would triumph. Psalm 84 mentions the city of Mecca (also known as Baca in the Quran and to Muslims and Arabs before Islam) by name:

4 Blessed are those who live in your house. They are always praising you. Selah

5 Blessed are those whose strength comes from you. They have decided to travel to your temple.

6 As they pass through the dry Valley of Baca, they make it a place where water flows. The rain in the fall covers it with pools. (Psalm 84)

These verses speak of the dry valley of Baca and of the Kaba[20] and describe the well of Zamzam that continues to flow today.

The well of Zamzam was first miraculously started by the strike of the foot of baby Ishmael when he nearly died of thirst. His mother Hagar prayed to Yahweh while running between two hills known as Safa and Marwah. When she finished the seventh run between the two hills, she noticed that her baby's cries had ceased and upon examination she found flowing water gushing from under his foot. Muslims repeat the actions of Hagar until this day when they make their trip to Mecca to perform the pilgrimage. They also drink the water of Zamzam and make sure to bring some back home as a prized and holy gift, for they consider Zamzam to be a living miracle of God.

---

20. the house of worship first built by angels for Adam and Eve and restored by Abraham and Ishmael

Prophet Muhammad's Name

Jews and Christians also found the prophet's name in their scriptures. In the Song of Solomon 5:16 it says:

חִכּוֹ, מַמְתַקִּים, וְכֻלּוֹ, מַחֲמַדִּים: זֶה דוֹדִי וְזֶה רֵעִי, בְּנוֹת יְרוּשָׁלִָם

Transliteration: Hakku mumitaqim wa kullu MAKHAMMADIM zah dawadee wa zah ra'ayee, banuwt Yerushalem.

The literal and figurative translation of this verse into the English language is: "His speech is most sweet, he is completely Muhammad, one out to another as a love-token from one out to another, my fellow friend, O you Daughters of Jerusalem."

However, the King James Version of the Bible reports the verse as follows: "His mouth is most sweet; yea, he is altogether lovely. This is my beloved, and this is my friend, O daughters of Jerusalem." In the Hebrew language, *im* is added for respect. Similarly *im* is added after the name of Prophet Muhammad in the above passage rendering it *Muhammadim*. In English translations, the name Muhammad was translated as "altogether lovely," but in the Old Testament in Hebrew, the name of Prophet Muhammad is yet present.

It is truly unfortunate that the name was not reported as it is in English Bibles, for it is a clear violation of literary integrity to translate names. A man whose name is Mr. Green would take on an entirely different character if he is described as "having the color of plants" instead of maintaining "Green" as his name. In fact, the entire meaning of the passage and the message would change if such a translation were to be made. This is indeed what resulted in the above-mentioned passage when the name Muhammad was translated into "he is altogether lovely" instead of being kept as a name, Muhammad.

Blessing for Ishmael

The lineage of Prophet Muhammad traces back to Ishmael, Abraham's first-born. Indeed, God's covenant and promise to Abraham to bless his children was fulfilled with the blessing of Isaac and his descendants. Yet, per the scriptures, the covenant and promise were fulfilled with Abraham's first-born (Ishmael) and his descendants. Genesis speaks of God's promise to Abraham and his descendants before any child was born to him:

I will make you into a great nation. I will bless you. I will make your name great. You will be a blessing to others. I will bless those who bless you. I will put a curse on anyone who calls down a curse on you. All nations on earth will be blessed because of you. (Genesis 12:2–3)

Genesis 17:4 reiterates God's promise after the birth of Ishmael and before the birth of Isaac. Later in the Book of Genesis, Isaac is specifically blessed, as was Ishmael. Both were promised by God to become "a great nation" ("I will make the son of your servant into a nation also." Genesis 21:13).

According to Deuteronomy 21:15–17, the traditional rights and privileges of the first-born son are not to be affected by the social status of his mother.[21] This is consistent with the moral and humanitarian principles of Judaism, Christianity, and Islam.

The full legitimacy of Ishmael as Abraham's son and "seed" and the full legitimacy of his mother, Hagar, as Abraham's wife, are clearly stated in Genesis 21:13 and 16:3. After Jesus, the last Israelite messenger and prophet, it was time that God's promise to bless Ishmael and his

---

21. Being a "free" woman such as Sarah, Isaac's mother, or a "bondwoman" such as Hagar, Ishmael's mother

descendants be fulfilled. Less than 600 years after Jesus came the last messenger of God, Muhammad, from the progeny of Abraham through Ishmael. God's blessing of both of the main branches of Abraham's family tree was now fulfilled.

Awaited Prophet From Arabia

The Old Testament clearly states that the awaited prophet was to come from Arabia. Deuteronomy 33:1-2 combines references to Moses, Jesus, and Muhammad. It speaks of God (i.e., God's revelation) coming from Sinai, rising from Seir (perhaps the village of Sair near Jerusalem), and shining forth from Paran. According to Genesis 21:21, the wilderness of Paran was the place where Ishmael settled, specifically in Mecca, Arabia.

The King James version of the Bible mentions the pilgrims passing through the valley of Baca (another name of Mecca) in Psalm 84:4-6, and Isaiah 42:1-13 speaks of the beloved of God, His elect and messenger, who will bring down a law to be awaited in the isles and who "shall not fail nor be discouraged till he have set judgment on earth." Verse 11 connects that awaited one with the descendants of Kedar. Kedar, according to Genesis 25:13, was the second son of Ishmael, the ancestor of Prophet Muhammad.

As for Medina, Habakkuk 3:3 speaks of God (God's help) coming from Teman (an oasis north of Medina according to J. Hasting's Dictionary of the Bible), and the holy one (coming) from Paran. That holy one was Prophet Muhammad who, under persecution, migrated from Paran (Mecca) to be received enthusiastically in Medina.

Indeed, the story of the migration of the Prophet and his persecuted followers is vividly described in Isaiah 21:13-17. Those verses also foretold the Battle of Badr, on the outskirts of Medina, in which the few ill-armed faithful miraculously defeated the "mighty" men of

Kedar who sought to destroy Islam and intimidate their own folk who had become Muslims.

Prophet Like Unto Moses

The prophet "like unto Moses" from the "brethren" of the Israelites (i.e., from the Ishmaelites) was described as one in whose mouth God will put His words and that he will speak in the name of God:

> I will raise them up a prophet from among their brethren, like unto thee; and I will put my words in his mouth, and he shall speak unto them all that I shall command him. And it shall come to pass, that whosoever will not hearken unto my words which he shall speak in my name, I will require it of him. (Deuteronomy 18:18–19)

Trinitarian Christians contend that this prophecy refers to Jesus because Jesus was like Moses—after all, Moses was a Jew, as was Jesus. Moses was a prophet, as was Jesus. However, if these two are the only criteria for this prophecy to be fulfilled, then all the prophets of the Bible who came after Moses such as Solomon, Isaiah, Ezekiel, Daniel, Hosea, Joel, Malachi, and John the Baptist would fulfill this prophecy given that all were Jews as well as prophets.

It is Prophet Muhammad who is more like Moses for both had a father and a mother while Jesus was born miraculously without a father,[22] and they both were married and had children while Jesus, according to the Bible, did not marry nor had he any children. Furthermore, both Moses and Muhammad died natural deaths, but Jesus has been raised up alive according to the Quran (4:157–158) or was crucified according to Trinitarian Christians.

---

22. Matthew 1:18 and Luke 1:35 and also the Quran 3:42–47

Twelve Princes

Genesis 17:20 explains how God promised the continuation of the blessing of Ishmael by the eventual bringing about of twelve princes who would become a great nation:

▼

As for Ishmael, I have heard you; behold, I will bless him, and will make him fruitful and will multiply him exceedingly. He shall become the father of twelve princes, and I will make him a great nation. (Genesis 17:20)
▲

This prophecy was fulfilled through the twelve imams who descended from Prophet Muhammad and who were foretold by him.

An Unlearned Prophet

Yet, perhaps one of the most telling passages in the English Bible is that mentioned in the Book of Isaiah: "And the book is delivered to him that is not learned, saying, Read this, I pray thee: and he saith, I am not learned" (Isaiah 29:12). This prophecy was perfectly fulfilled when Prophet Muhammad received the first revelation when Archangel Gabriel appeared to him in the cave. Gabriel commanded him by saying "Read (*iqra*). Prophet Muhammad replied, "I am not learned."

The Comforter

The verses discussed are but a few of the verses Muslims cite demonstrating how the Old Testament prophesied the coming of Muhammad as a prophet. The New Testament contains similar passages that Muslims contend clearly foretell the coming of Islam as promised by God. The Quran states:

And remember, Jesus, the son of Mary, said, "O Children of
Israel! I am the messenger of Allah (sent) to you, confirming
the Law (which came) before me and giving glad tidings of a
messenger to come after me, whose name shall be Ahmed."
But when he came to them with clear signs, they said, "This
is evident sorcery!" (Quran 61:6)

Spirit of truth, not Holy Ghost

It is reported in John 15:26 that Jesus said, "But when the Comforter
is come, whom I will send unto you from the Father, even the Spirit
of truth, which proceedeth from the Father, he shall testify of me."
While the Comforter (Paraclete in some translations) is described as
the spirit of truth (whose meaning coincides with Muhammad's famous
title *al-Amin,* the Trustworthy), he is identified in one verse as the
Holy Ghost (John 14:26). Such a designation is, however, inconsistent
with the profile of that Comforter. In the words of the Dictionary of
the Bible (Ed. J. Mackenzie) "These items, it must be admitted, do not
give an entirely coherent picture."

A human who speaks revelation

According to John 16:12–14, Jesus said, "I have yet many things to say
unto you, but ye cannot bear them now. Howbeit when he, the Spirit
of truth is come, he will guide you unto all truth: for he shall not speak
of himself; but whatsoever he shall hear, that shall he speak: and he
will show you things to come. He shall glorify me." It is clear that the
Comforter is a male human being ("*he* shall speak"). Muslims say it
refers to Muhammad. He was illiterate and received God's revelation
through Archangel Gabriel and conveyed it by word of mouth. And
Prophet Muhammad testified to the prophethood of Jesus.

Jesus must go away

In John 16:7, it states, "Nevertheless I tell you the truth; it is expedient for you that I go away: for if I go not away, the Comforter will not come unto you; but if I depart, I will send him unto you." Trinitarian Christians say that the Comforter mentioned in these prophecies refers to the Holy Spirit. However, Muslims argue that the prophecy clearly states that only if Jesus departs will the Comforter come. The Bible states that the Holy Spirit was already present on Earth before and during the time of Jesus, in the womb of Elizabeth, and again when Jesus was being baptized. Hence this prophecy refers to another being and not to the Holy Spirit.

Abiding with us forever

In John 14:16, Jesus is reported to have said, "And I will pray the Father, and he shall give you another Comforter, that he may abide with you forever." How, then, does Prophet Muhammad abide with us forever? The answer to this lies in the Jewish teaching that a man lives forever through his sons. Indeed, Prophet Muhammad named the twelve imams from his descendants who will carry the message of God until the return of Jesus.

The Awaited Prophet

Up to the time of Jesus, the Israelites were still awaiting that prophet like unto Moses prophesied in Deuteronomy 18:18. When John the Baptist came, they asked him if he was Christ and he said "no." They asked him if he was Elias and he said "no." Then, in apparent reference to Deuteronomy 18:18, they asked him, "Art thou that Prophet," and he answered "No" (John 1: 19-21). It is clear from their question that Christ and "that Prophet" are not the same person and John the Baptist denies being either of them. So who was that prophet?

Muslims contend it is Muhammad. He was the Paraclete or Comforter (helper) sent by God after Jesus Christ. Muhammad testified of Jesus, taught new things which could not be borne at Jesus' time, spoke what he heard (revelation), dwelled with the believers (through his progeny), and told of many things to come which "came to pass" while he was still alive and after he died.

Conclusion

It is evident to religious scholars that Prophet Muhammad was foretold in the Old and New Testaments. As stated above, these prophecies were well-known to both Jewish and Christian contemporaries of the eras preceding and coinciding with the advent of Islam.

These prophecies were the clear motivation of three Jewish tribes and Christian scholars in seeking Mecca and Medina as their places of residence in awaiting the coming of the new prophet. Because of the clarity and presence of such clear references in the Holy Book to the coming of Islam, perhaps this can be a natural starting point where the followers of the three faiths can converge. After all, wouldn't the acceptance of Muhammad's prophecy be a fulfillment of both Jewish and Christian prophecies? Thus a strengthening of their faiths?

Chapter Seven

Jihad and the Morality of War

Islamic canonical experts are faced with a myriad of issues today that did not exist prior to the vast advancements in technology and weaponry. There have always been clear foundations in Islamic teachings that define when Muslims may engage in war (albeit with some differences between Shia and Sunni interpretations of these rules) but stark differences in the understanding of how these rules should be implemented.

Furthermore, Islam has clearly defined rules of engagement that cover the kind of weapons and methods that are allowed to be used when engaging an enemy, how to treat prisoners of war, and when and how to engage in war. The questions that face Islamic canonical experts do not center on the existence of such rulings but rather on how to apply these rules to contemporary challenges.

For example, Islam prohibits the use of poison in battlefields according to Ayatullah Khoei:

It is not permitted to use poison against the land of the polytheists because the Prophet Muhammad, peace be upon him and his progeny, ordered (the Muslims) not to do so according to the acceptable narration of the Sukuni who narrated that Abi Abdallah, peace be upon him, said that Amir Al-Momeneen, peace be upon him, said, "The Messenger of

Allah, peace be upon him and his progeny, prohibited the use
of poison against the land of the polytheists."[23]

So how does this statement apply to today's weaponry? Most weapons
used in modern warfare use some form of poison or fire.[24] Does
the prohibition to use poison apply to the prevention of the use of
chemical weapons? There is consensus among both Shia and Sunni
experts of Islamic canonical law that weapons of mass destruction
are prohibited because indiscriminant killing violates the foundation
of Islam's goal of saving humanity and human life. But are Muslims
allowed to own weapons of mass destruction for deterrent purposes
even if they never intend to use such weapons?

Additionally, globalization, which has emerged because of advancements
in information and transportation technologies, causes people from
around the world, including Muslims, to relocate to new areas. Islam
places special emphasis on upholding the tenets of contractual
obligations. A question that faces Muslim experts is whether entry
visas constitute such contracts that must be obeyed.

The discussion from a canonical expert viewpoint is not that of
political or moral nature, rather it is whether accepting to travel to
or to emigrate to a country that grants a visa constitutes religious
obligation to abide by all of the laws of that country. These questions
have far-reaching implications on how Muslim countries conduct their
policies and engage in wars and on how militant Islamic movements
carry out their operations outside of their geographical domains. We
shall attempt to address these questions in this chapter.

23. Ayatullah al-Khoei. n.d. Risalah, fatwa 54.
24. See Sunan Ibi Daoud under the prohibition to use fire to burn one's enemy
122:2675.

Interpreting Established Laws and Making New Laws in Shia Islam

Before explaining the basis for the contemporary understanding of war ethics in Shia Islam, one must form a clear picture of how Shia Muslims view Islamic laws and the necessity to abide by them.

Justice is fundamental

A fundamental theme of the Shia belief system is the justice of God. Shias believe that justice is one of the positive attributes of God and that this foundation affects everything from the sending of messengers and prophets to the essential existence of infallible interpreters of God's messages starting with Adam and running through the twelfth imam and his return with Jesus the Messiah.

This theme of the essentiality of justice in every aspect of human life transcends social and religious laws in the cultural psyche of Shia scholars and societies throughout the centuries and into the future. How Shias view war is heavily influenced by the justice theme. A scholarly understanding of the rules of war must be taken into account whenever a verdict is issued by any Shia scholar.

Interpreting laws and making new ones when the current imam is in occultation

The current rightful infallible leader of Muslims, according to Shia teachings, is the twelfth prince mentioned in Genesis 17:20.[25] He is called Imam Mahdi by Shia Muslims—*Imam* being a title for an infallible guide and *Mahdi* being a title meaning 'guided one.' He was

---

25. "As for Ishmael, I have heard you; behold, I will bless him, and will make him fruitful and will multiply him exceedingly. He shall become the father of twelve princes, and I will make him a great nation." (Genesis 17:20)

born in 869 CE and has been in occultation since he was 71 years old. He will come out of occultation to establish God's just kingdom on Earth with Jesus when God gives him permission to. He is not the first of God's messengers to disappear from our perception without dying. Enoch[26] and Elijah[27] in the Old Testament are said to have not died, and Muslims believe that Jesus has not died yet either although they believe Jesus is in a level of heaven and Imam Mahdi is on Earth.

Because the twelfth imam is in occultation, it is a part of the justice of God that qualified experts exist to interpret Islamic law and apply it to modern situations. This ensures that Muslims are able to understand and comply with the most accurate interpretation of these laws. For this reason, these qualified scholars, who must possess certain qualities to hold these important positions, are viewed as the twelfth imam's representatives.

The representatives differ on issues that relate to the occultation of the twelfth imam, such as whether Muslims may engage in pre-emptive or offensive wars. The majority view of Shia scholars is that only defensive wars are permitted during the period of occultation of the current imam. Where some of these scholars issued verdicts legalizing offensive wars, their views, upon further contemplation, show that their definition of offensive war falls, in fact, under the title of defensive war and that they reference instead initiating war for pre-emptive reasons only.

An individual's responsibility to choose and follow a just interpreter of Islamic law

Through an intricate system of investigation and research, every Shia Muslim is required to choose one from a handful of scholars as an ultimate reference on Islamic laws. Once the selection is made, this

---

26. Genesis 5:24
27. 2 Kings 2:11

scholar becomes the reference for the interpretation and execution of all laws for that individual. This scholarly designation is known as *marja*, which literally means 'reference,' and the act of following the interpretations of a *marja* is known as *taqlid* which translates into 'emulation.'

Taqlid can only be done in the interpretation and implementation of Islamic laws and is not permitted for articles of faith and understanding of God and the system of beliefs. Shia Muslims believe that every individual is required to employ all available methods to understand the oneness of God, the need for Judgement Day, prophets, imams, etc.

Only an average of less than ten scholars have ever qualified at any one point in time to reach a degree of knowledge and scrutiny to receive the degree of *marja* since the occultation of the twelfth imam. Today, there are tens of thousands of Shia scholars and less than ten *marjas*. Among them are the following:

- Grand Ayatullah Sayyid Ali Sistani
- Grand Ayatullah Ali Husayni Khamenei [28]
- Grand Ayatullah Nasar Makaram Shirazi
- Grand Ayatullah Sayyid Saeed Hakim
- Grand Ayatullah Jafar Subhani

Each one of these grand scholars (*marjas*) has studied each aspect of Islamic law for over thirty years and has taught other scholars in seminary for extended periods. The scholars who are the students of the grand scholars serve as the pastors (preachers) in Shia mosques. Each grand scholar must have the ability to derive verdicts (*fatwas*) from the main sources of Islamic law and publish a canonical book that contains their rulings. This book, which is found in every Shia household, is known as a *risalah* or a 'dispatch' as it is viewed as being dispatched from the grand scholar to his followers.

---

28. the supreme leader of the Islamic Republic of Iran at the time of this book's first publication

The authority of a just interpreter of Islamic law

Once a *fatwa* is issued, it is viewed as indisputable law for Muslims. A *fatwa* has such a great level of sanctity that believers do not question the obligation to adhere to it—not adhering to it means violating the teachings of Islam. Since the power of the grand scholar is derived from his authority as a representative of the twelfth imam, no other authority may challenge his interpretation, including governments and their branches.

It is because of this power that Ayatullah Khomeini was able to bring down the Shah of Iran, and it is because of this power that the government of Iran was not able to avert an international political crisis when Ayatullah Khomeini issued the verdict condemning Salman Rushdie in response to Rushdie's book *Satanic Verses.* Western governments put tremendous pressure on Iran's political leaders to "withdraw" the verdict when, in fact, Iran's political leaders had no authority to do so.

Therefore, a clear understanding of a verdict of a contemporary grand scholar regarding war is of paramount importance for clarity in how Shia Muslims view war in today's world. We shall examine these verdicts in this chapter.

Defensive War: The Only Basis for Fighting

Islam sanctions defensive war (*jihad*)[29] against oppressors in the absence of other means to eliminate injustice regardless of whether the oppressors are Muslims or otherwise. Islam does not permit war on anyone, Muslim or non-Muslim, for any other reason except as stated above. The following verses in the Holy Quran are referenced by Shia Muslim scholars to discuss the reasons for engaging in war

---

29. The greater struggle (greater *jihad*) of a Muslim is to be a good Muslim. The lesser *jihad* is to defend (as in war).

and their understanding of the type of war of which Muslims are permitted to partake:

Those who are fought against are permitted [to fight] because they have been wronged, and Allah is indeed able to help them. Those who were expelled from their homes unjustly, only because they said, "Allah is our Lord." Had not Allah repulsed the people from one another, ruin would have befallen the monasteries, churches, synagogues and mosques in which Allah's Name is mentioned greatly. Allah will surely help those who help Him. Indeed Allah is all-strong, all-mighty. Those who, if We granted them power in the land, maintain the prayer, give the zakat, and bid what is right and forbid what is wrong. And with Allah rests the outcome of all matters. (Quran 22:39–41)

These verses from the Holy Quran constitute the foundation for the philosophy of war according to modern day Muslim scholars. Nearly all Shia scholars focus their study of whether Muslim governments may engage in war on these verses.

Ayatullah Khoei, a leading Muslim scholar who lived in Najaf, Iraq, held a minority view among Shia scholars that these verses give permission to Muslim governments to initiate war. Even his interpretation does not, in its essence, depart from the defensive posture that the majority of scholars understand these verses to give.

Verse 22:39 of the Holy Quran ("Those who are fought against are permitted [to fight] because they have been wronged, and Allah is indeed able to help them") clearly states that permission is given to Muslims to fight only after war has been waged against them. The default rule is that war is prohibited, and permission is needed to engage in it. The verse does not call for the initiation of war. Imam Ali (peace be upon him), the prophet's cousin and the first of the twelve imams according to Shia teachings, ordered his commanders not to fire the first arrow in any battle he waged.

When the second imam (a disciple of Muhammad), Hussain (peace be upon him), was surrounded in Karbala, Iraq by 4000 soldiers, he ordered his seventy-two companions not to fire the first arrow. Shia scholars understand those actions to stem from the above-mentioned verses. Therefore, scholars agree that war in Islam must be of defensive nature.

The terrorists who perpetrated the September 11, 2001 attacks claimed that Muslims were attacked and that they were only fighting back. However, we shall find that the definition of being attacked first did not apply to their situation, and, furthermore, we will prove that they violated the rules of engagement as outlined by Islamic teachings when they carried out their heinous crime.

Having to have been wronged first

Another clear condition for permission to engage in war is that Muslims must be wronged before they may engage in war. Muslim scholars understand this verse to require that a Muslim government must not be on the wrong side of a dispute in order for Muslims to support its war efforts. The verse says, "because they have been wronged," and it continues to say, "and Allah is indeed able to help them." This promise to come to the aid of Muslims requires them to be right in their dispute. All Muslims agree that God is just and so He would not take the side of the transgressor. Therefore, when Muslims are given permission to engage in defensive war, another condition for this permission is that they must not have transgressed another party which caused it to wage war against Muslims in the first place.

Chapter 2, verse 190 of the Holy Quran lays out this argument more clearly: "Fight in the way of Allah those who fight you, but do not transgress. Indeed Allah does not like transgressors." That transgression applies not only to fighting defensively but also to creating the cause of transgression in the first place.

Some Muslim scholars (both Shia and Sunni) argue that the causes of transgression are created when another party meddles directly or indirectly in the affairs of Muslims; therefore, Muslim governments are given permission in these cases to initiate war as this, they argue, is defensive and not offensive war.

Who gives authority to engage in war?

The late Ayatullah Khoei states in his *risalah*, in the section "Ordering Good and Forbidding Evil," that war (lesser *jihad*) is a collective obligation. It is not obligatory on any individual Muslim unless the imam of the present day[30] issues such a decree. Reference to the Imam in this verdict clearly proves that Khoei's intention is that *jihad* remain a collective obligation—meaning that it is not the personal obligation of any Muslim (unless the infallible imam who is in occultation issues such a decree to the contrary).

Ayatullah Khoei further makes it a condition that during the occultation of the infallible imam, only a qualified Muslim scholar with certain qualifications may decide to engage in any form of war and, even then, he must consult with other experts before issuing such a decree. He further explains why only a qualified Islamic scholar with certain conditions may undertake the making of such conditions, "If anyone who does not meet these requirements issues such a decree, this will lead to chaos and injustices and the improper implementation (of these rules)."[31]

This ruling by Ayatullah Khoei therefore prohibits secular leaders of all Muslim governments from initiating or leading wars under any circumstances except when the very existence of Islam is at stake. In

---

30. Imam Mahdi, the twelfth imam (may God hasten his return)
31. Ayatullah al-Khoei. n.d. Risalah, p. 366.

verdict number 20 of his *risalah*, Ayatullah Khoei further restates a ruling on which nearly all Muslim scholars, Shia and Sunni, agree. He writes, "it is not permitted to engage the infidels after giving them a promise of safety or entering into a truce with them, as this would be a violation of both which is not permitted."

Some Muslim experts understood Ayatullah Khoei's stance on war to permit the start of offensive wars. Careful analysis of his view shows that his intention is that such war may be started only under such extreme conditions—as when the existence of Islam is at stake. A careful reading of the following verdict shows that if Islam's existence is not at stake, then the twelfth imam's presence is a requirement for engaging in war.

> It is obligatory on every Muslim to defend the faith of Islam if it is subject to danger (*maaredh al-khatar*, meaning 'for its existence') and the permission of the Imam, peace be upon him, is not required, without doubt, and there is no disagreement in this regard. There is no difference in this regard whether the Imam was present or is in occultation.[32]

Ayatullah Fadl-Allah, another leading grand scholar and student of Khoei, further supports this understanding when he issued a verdict stating that only defensive wars are allowed during the time of occultation and that preventive war (starting war when an attack on Muslims is about to happen) belongs to the category of defensive war.

Having to have a legitimate government established

Another aspect of engagement in war that is discussed when these verses are mentioned is that Muslims may only wage war if a just,

---

32. Ayatullah al-Khoei. n.d. Risalah.

Islamic, legitimate government is established. Shia scholars are unanimous in this view. The only other condition whereby Muslim individuals or groups are allowed to engage in war is when the very existence of Islam is in danger and a legitimate Muslim authority cannot exist under those circumstances.

Verse 22:41 of the Holy Quran states that permission to fight back is given to those who meet the following condition: "Those who, if We granted them power in the land." This verse is understood to indicate that permission is given to Muslims to engage in war if the establishment of such authority is based on Islamic principles.

This view is not shared by all Muslim schools of thought. Shaykh Faysal Mawlawi, a known Sunni scholar and deputy head of the European Council for Fatwa and Research, argues that Sunni Muslims are permitted to come to the aide of Hezbollah, a Shia organization, because, according to him, "The majority of scholars agree that it is permitted to fight under the banner of an army leader even if he is a transgressor, unjust, or a sinner." He supports his view by citing major Sunni sources.

Shia scholars, on the other hand, contend that a leader who is not righteous is bound to make false judgements that are contradictory to justice and will, therefore, inevitably start or engage in wars based on those misjudgments. This view, however, does not absolve Shia Muslims from praying for those who wrongfully engage in war to be guided and does not absolve them from attempting to persuade others to change their ways.

War in Prophet Muhammad's time

The three Quranic verses regarding war that we are discussing were revealed during the second year after the Muslims emigrated to Medina upon the first confrontation of war against them. This confrontation placed the young Muslim nation in a defensive situation. During the prior thirteen years, Muslims were subjected to all forms of torture, besiegement, deportation, and aggression by those who opposed the rising influence of a monotheistic faith that challenged the status quo. The faithful repeatedly asked Prophet Muhammad for permission to fight back, but he refused. Fighting violates the very essence of the message he was sent to deliver and the meaning of the name given to this message by God, *Islam*. Since the lingual foundation of the word *islam* is 'peace' and 'submission,' fighting is inconsistent with the message.

In addition, Muslims were few in number and had few or no means of fighting back. Therefore, Prophet Muhammad ordered a select group of Muslims to seek refuge in Africa where a devout Christian king, known as Nagos, ruled with fairness. This move had deep implications for how Muslims should conduct themselves throughout all times including our current situation.

Prophet Muhammad did not permit Muslims to fight back if they could avoid violence, if they did not have the means for self-defense, or if they could align themselves with a monotheistic power. Sects within Islam that endorse assassinations or indiscriminate mass murder do so based on their own personal judgements and are in clear violation of the Prophet's own conduct and clear Islamic teachings.

Two more reasons for defensive war

Turning our attention back to the details of the three verses addressing war, we find the following two additional conditions for Muslims to engage in defensive war:

- If Muslims are expelled from their land, then they are permitted to fight back.

- If any monotheists are expelled from their land for worshipping God, then Muslims must fight defensively on the side of the expelled people.

Muslims expelled from their land

Verse 22:40 mentions another logical foundation for the legitimacy of engaging in defensive war: If Muslims are expelled from their land, then they are permitted to fight back. The word 'homes' stated in the verse is a valiant effort to translate the Arabic word *diyarehim* which includes all that is inhabited by people, such as houses, lands, and countries. Again, the condition for those Muslims who have been expelled from their lands to fight back is that they have been made to leave their lands unjustly. It can be said, therefore, that if Muslims occupy others' lands without a legitimate reason, then the Muslims do not have the right to engage in war defensively when the people try to get their land back. They must withdraw from the lands they are occupying.

It is further understood that Muslims are not permitted to come to the aid of a group of Muslims who transgress against others or unjustly occupy land. Conversely, when Muslim lands are unjustly occupied by others, they must fight back and come to the aid of those Muslims who have been wronged.

The Palestinian population often relies on these verses from the Holy Quran to rally their Muslim brethren around the world to come to their aid. During the onset of the conflict when the United Kingdom gave Palestine to the Jews, Palestinians rallied the rest of the Muslim world under the leadership of Islamic movements. Later, during the fifties and sixties, when the Palestine Liberation Organization (PLO) came to exist, it adopted a nationalistic ideology and abandoned the Islamic approach, relying instead on support from the Soviet Union and China, both atheistic powers.

The PLO further turned to its Arab brethren for aid and support and downplayed offers of support from other Muslim nations and individuals. This strategy continued until other competing movements in Palestine came to exist with Islamic ideologies. The Muslim Brotherhood, which was fiercely opposed by the secular PLO, was finally successful in creating a movement that came to play a major role in the Middle East conflict, Hamas.

Monotheists expelled from their land for worshipping God

Verse 22:40 continues on to reveal yet another very important aspect of legitimizing the engagement in defensive war—protecting the freedom to worship, with special emphasis on *monotheists*, not Muslims only. God says that when people are expelled from their lands because they say "our Lord is Allah," then those people must defend themselves, and Muslims must come to their aid.

This verse gives an indication that monotheism will be the target of transgression. Some scholars understand the words 'Allah is our Lord' to include all monotheists and not just Muslims.[33] The words 'our Lord,' a translation from the Arabic word *rabuna*, mean that the issuers of the statement 'Allah is our Lord' believe that God is the only God and only sustainer.

In other words, they believe in 'one God one Lord' as this is the deeply held belief of all Muslims. However, this statement, it can be argued, is also held as the belief of other groups like some Christian and Jewish sects. The rest of the verse 22:40 lists mosques *after* mentioning other places of worship that do not belong to Muslims. Surely, monasteries and churches are known places of worship of the followers of Christ, while synagogues are the recognized temples of the Jewish people. The stated purpose of defending these places of worship is to defend the remembrance of God's name in them.

The Prophet of Islam made it clear that if any member of the engaged enemy armies declares that there is only one God, then his life and property become protected, and he must not be harmed.[34] This

---

33. Fatwas by Fadl-Allah, section 10, page 1.
34. Sunan Ibi Daoud. 104:2624. n.d.

statement supports the view that the practices of monotheists are protected by Islam's defensive laws in the same way that Islam's own practices are and that Islam focuses on protecting monotheism whether practiced by Muslims or non-Muslims.

Illegal Early Conquests in the Name of Islam

Shia Muslim scholars contend that the Muslim conquests after Prophet Muhammad died were not compliant with Islamic teachings. Imam Ali[35] did not agree with occupying the lands of others for the sake of expansion. He did not participate in wars where the early Muslims sent armies to conquer new lands. This is despite the fact that Imam Ali himself was the de facto hero of all of the defensive wars in which Muslims engaged, in and around Mecca and Medina, when Prophet Muhammad was alive. This can be viewed as a rejection of the legitimacy of those conquests.

When Prophet Muhammad was sent to deliver the message of Islam, the first recipients of his divine message were nomadic tribes that considered each other's properties as fair bounty. Islam eradicated numerous ill habits such as revenge killings, the unfair treatment of women and minorities, adultery, and many others.

Unfortunately, not all of those who embraced the message of Islam did so because they believed it to be the rightly sent message from God. When Mecca fell to the Muslims in 630 CE, Prophet Muhammad gave amnesty to all the people of the city. Many decided to call themselves Muslims to partake in the new power and to position themselves and their tribes to take leadership positions in future generations. These new Muslims had heard Prophet Muhammad make many prophecies that all came to fruition. They also heard

---

35. the first of the twelve imams according to Shia teachings who were supposed to rule after Prophet Muhammad's death

75

him prophesize that the Muslims shall come to rule the lands of the Roman and Persian empires.

Many, like the Umayyad tribe, were in fierce competition with other Meccan tribes and wanted to share this future leadership. Therefore, after the death of Prophet Muhammad, some of these Muslim leaders wanted to expand their empires to increase their tribes' wealth and, in many cases, to keep their political opponents and the general Muslim public from objecting to their mishandling of the treasury.

Of course Muslims would not fight for the sake of increasing the wealth of these tribes, so these leaders either changed the interpretation of some Islamic teachings to suit their goals or simply hired narrators who fabricated narrations and attributed them to Prophet Muhammad.

Narrations are statements Prophet Muhammad is said to have made— statements that were not revelation from God. But because he was a prophet, all statements he made were in agreement with God's intention, and, therefore, if we knew for sure exactly what Prophet Muhammad had said, we could use his statements to know God's will.

Narrations in Islam are not a part of scripture like they are in Christianity. The gospels in the New Testament are the equivalent of narrations in Islam. The gospels contain statements Jesus is said to have made, but textual analysis of New Testament manuscripts supports the view that some verses are very likely additions to the text. In Luke 22 in the scene of the Lord's Supper, the parts "Which has been given for you; do this in remembrance of me" (in verse 19) and "this cup is the new covenant in my blood which is shed for you" (in verse 20) were likely additions to scripture by scribes.[36] The last twelve verses of Mark are said to have been added by scribes as well (Mark 16:9–20).[37] These verses talk about Jesus appearing to Mary

---

36. Bart D. Ehrman, *Misquoting Jesus: the story behind who changed the Bible and why,* (New York: Harper, San Francisco, 2005), 166, Kindle file.
37. Ibid. 66.

Magdalene and two disciples and the Great Commission. Narrations in Islam are subject to modification and complete fabrication as well—that's why students in Shia Islamic seminaries have a whole field that teaches how to ascertain the authenticity of a narration.

The leaders who pronounced faith in Islam solely to increase their wealth and influence understood the effect they could have on people's faith if they could pass off a made-up narration as an authentic one. They succeeded in causing some Muslims to believe the made-up narrations thus causing them to cling to false teachings not knowing their error.

When these leaders found their armies in control of lands that did not bring them wealth, they simply withdrew their armies and left the original inhabitants behind, caring not if they embraced Islam or continued to worship multiple idols.

Additionally, history recorded many instances where the Umayyad armies refused to accept the inhabitants of newly occupied territories as Muslims and instead insisted that they pay tax. This clearly exhibits their true motives for those conquests—money and not the expansion of the faith of Islam.

Islam Spreads by Trading

A study of the quality of Muslims since the times of the conquests finds two outstanding facts. One is that the vast majority of people who embraced Islam did so by interacting with Muslims, not by war. Indonesia and Malaysia who are hosts to the largest Muslim populations both embraced Islam by trading with Muslim merchants. Africa and southern Europe, which were conquered by the early Muslim armies, had smaller numbers of Muslims compared to these two countries.

It is only since the twentieth century that Islam took a strong foothold in the African continent south of the desert, which is largely inhabited by the descendants of early Muslims. This conversion to Islam by Sub-

Saharan Africa only occurred when Africans traded and interacted with the rest of the Muslim world and not because of conquests.

The second outstanding observation is that the quality of Muslims who embraced Islam by interacting with Muslims is that of moderation and adherence.

Islam Prohibits Compulsion in Faith

Ayatullah Muhammad Hussain Tabatabai, perhaps the greatest philosopher and Quran expert of all times, cites Quranic verse 22:40 as evidence that Islam prohibits compulsion in faith and that the main reason behind legislating war in Islam is to protect monotheism—whether it be practiced by Muslims or non-Muslims:

It is one of the verses that shows that Islam is not based on the sword and killing and that it does not allow Muslims to compel or coerce others to accept Islam. It is contrary to the view held by many Muslims and non-Muslims alike that Islam is the religion of the sword. They bring as their evidence the legislation of jihad which is one of the pillars of Islam.

We have already clarified, while writing the commentary on the verses of fighting, that the fighting ordained by Islam is neither for the purpose of material advancement nor for spreading the religion by force. It was ordained only for reviving the truth and defending the most precious treasure of nature—the faith of monotheism. Where monotheism is accepted by the people—even if they remain Jew or Christian—Islam does not fight with them. Therefore, the objection arises from clouded thinking.

The verse "There is no compulsion in religion (Quran 2:256)," is not abrogated by the verse of the sword, although some writers think so. The order is followed by its reason: "truly the right way has become clearly distinct from error (Quran 2:257)," Such an order cannot be cancelled unless and until its reason is abrogated. So as long as the reason is valid the rule must remain valid. There is no need to emphasize that the verse of the sword cannot negate the clear distinction of the right way from error. For example, the verses "and kill them wherever you find them" (Quran 4:89) and "And fight in the way of Allah" (Quran 2:190), have no effect whatsoever on the clear distinction of truth from falsehood; and therefore they cannot abrogate an order based on that distinction.

In other words, this order is because the right way is made clearly distinct from error. Moreover, this distinction is as valid after the revelation of the verses of fighting as it was before that. The cause is not changed, the effect, that is, the said order, cannot be changed or cancelled.[38]

The Expected Result of Engaging in Defensive War

The three Quranic verses we are discussing describe those who are given permission to fight back as possessing a quality that illustrates their expected intention for engaging in war—they must establish a sound moral and economic system to support the society for which they fight. Quranic verse 22:41 highlights three basic foundations: "They are those who, if We establish them in the land, establish regular prayer, give regular charity, enjoin the right and forbid wrong." The three foundations are 1) establishing regular prayer, 2) giving regular charity, and 3) enjoining the right and forbidding wrong.

---

38. Abu al-Fath Abd al-Rahman al-Mansur al-Khazini, *Mizan al-Hikamah,* vol. 4. 1121 CE.

Establishing regular prayer

In Islam, there is no other ritual that is as fundamental to the Islamic way of worship and life as prayer. Muslims are required to perform five prayers a day. They may do so individually; however, great emphasis is placed on performing these prayers in congregation. This is in addition to the weekly Friday prayer, which is required to be congregational, and the annual prayers of religious holidays, which are also required to be congregational. During these congregational prayers, the prayer leader must deliver two speeches and one must focus on current issues facing the community. There are strict rules governing the distance between where these prayers are held so that the largest number of worshippers may gather to share the same outcome.

Prayer has an individual dimension for the betterment of society's members as well as a deep societal foundation that encompasses spirituality, politics, and unity. This emphasis can be seen when Muslims are required to recite the same words at the same time while physically synchronizing their prayers and facing the same direction, which is towards the Kaba. They must all stand together, bend together, and prostrate themselves behind the prayer leader together.

The impact of such ritual then takes on far-reaching implications for Muslims. Muslims learn how to conduct themselves in the same physical and spiritual manner throughout the ages. When Muslims adhere to these requirements, they come to share a moral framework that extends beyond the limits of human-made laws and employ their spiritual and moral dimension to create a harmonious community.

Giving regular charity

The second foundation is that of socio-economic importance—to give regular charity. The goal of every successful economic system is to eliminate poverty and create equality between people while allowing individual effort to be rewarded. The Quran is a text that deals with moral issues; therefore, it is only appropriate that it start with the purpose of a successful economic system in mind—to eliminate poverty.

If the Quran were strictly an economics book, it may have started by explaining the merits and requirements of the Islamic economic system and detailing the various elements of this system. From the Quran's point of view, if all members of the society can achieve economic well-being because of spiritually influenced actions that lead to financial sufficiency, then Islam's economic system achieves its goal. Charity can only be given effectively if the socio-economic system is sound enough to allow for the creation of a philanthropic segment of the society. Perhaps then it can be derived that the expectation of those charged with defending the society is to create an economic system based on Islamic teachings that allows the giving of charity to found a balanced distribution of financial well-being.

Enjoining good and forbidding wrong

The third foundation, enjoining the right and forbidding wrong, is of penal and legal importance. It is one of the branches of religion (practices) according to Shia Islam's teachings. Enjoining good requires Muslims to remind everyone to conduct himself or herself in the best manner. Forbidding wrong is the compulsory act of attempting to prevent all acts that bring harm to an individual or the society. This is the basis for Islam's penal law.

Quranic verse 22:41 therefore exhibits the natural expectation of those who implement the Quran's requirement for self-defense—they must establish a governmental system that complies with Islam's teachings.

The three parameters given above encompass individual and collective spirituality, economic well-being, and a sound and sustainable legal system that encourages moral and positive conduct while countering those who are deemed harmful to the society and its individual members.

Polytheists Versus "People of the Book"

The word for 'polytheists'

At the heart of modern day strife between the West and Muslim insurgency is the defining of Western powers as representing polytheists or *mushrikin*.

> Those who disbelieve from among the followers of the Book do not like, nor do the polytheists, that the good should be sent down to you from your Lord, and Allah chooses especially whom He pleases for His mercy, and Allah is the Lord of mighty grace. (Quran 2:105)

The Arabic origin of the word *mushrikin*, 'polytheists', is *shirk* which means 'associating others with God.' There is not a doctrine that violates the very essence of Islam's foundation as does associating others with God. The word *islam* itself, 'submission to the one God,' loses its meaning if there is any form of *shirk* involved. *Mushrikin* are those who associate others with God. There is no tolerance for *shirk* in the Holy Quran.

> Indeed Allah does not forgive that any partner should be ascribed to Him, but He forgives anything besides that to whomever He wishes. And whoever ascribes partners to Allah has indeed fabricated [a lie] in great sinfulness. (Quran 4:48)

Mercy is the most practical relationship between humans and God, and this mercy reaches every aspect of human error or transgression including Adam and Eve eating from the tree. Islam teaches that God forgave them for doing so. Opposite *shirk* is *tawhid* which is acknowledging and accepting that there is only one God. The Quran states that God forgives all sins except that of associating others with God as it violates the foundation of the oneness of God.

The phrase for 'People of the Book'

Those among Muslims who do not have a scholarly understanding of the Quran often find it difficult to distinguish between two different terms that are used in its text. One is *mushrikin*, which we just discussed, and the other is *ahl al-kitab*. Some Muslims view the two groups of people referred to by these terms as one and the same while the Quran treats the two groups as separate entities requiring different rules of treatment by Muslims.

Mushrikin means 'polytheists.' Most Muslims believe *ahl al-kitab*, the 'People of the Book,' to be Jews and Christians. Other Muslims' understanding includes followers of other religions if their followers received a book from God through a messenger. While *mushrikin* is a term that was given to the people of Mecca who worshipped idols and gave them divine roles, *ahl al-kitab* was used early on in the Quran to distinguish the Jews and Christians who inhabited the Arabian Peninsula.

How the Quran says to treat People of the Book

This is not to say, however, that the Quran forgave some of the actions of the People of the Book. The basis of how to engage the People of the Book is laid out in the following verse:

> Say, "O People of the Book! Come to a word common between us and you: that we will worship no one but Allah, and that we will not ascribe any partner to Him, and that we will not take each other as lords besides Allah." But if they turn away,

say, "Be witnesses that we are muslims [those who have submitted to Allah]." (Quran 3:64)

God does not require the People of the Book to necessarily embrace Islam but asks them to return to pure monotheism. Monotheism would place Muslims and non-Muslim monotheists on an equal legal field in all of their worldly affairs thus allowing for the creation of an equitable society.

The Quran criticizes Christians for adopting the doctrine of the trinity and considers it a form of polytheism.

They are certainly faithless who say, "Allah is the Messiah, son of Mary." But the Messiah had said, "O Children of Israel! Worship Allah, my Lord and your Lord. Indeed whoever ascribes partners to Allah, Allah shall forbid him [entry into] paradise, and his refuge shall be the Fire, and the wrongdoers will not have any helpers." (Quran 5:72)

However, it is notable that the Quran encourages the Jews and Christians to adhere to their original revealed books, for in doing so, they would live according to the tenets of monotheism.

Let the people of the Evangel judge by what Allah has sent down in it. Those who do not judge by what Allah has sent down—it is they who are the transgressors. (Quran 5:47)

In verse 2:93, God rebukes those among the Jews who refused to obey Moses and issues a stern warning to them.

And when We took covenant with you and raised the Mount above you [declaring], "Hold on with power to what We have given you, and listen!" They said, "We hear, and disobey," and their hearts had been imbued with [the love of] the Calf, due to their faithlessness. Say, "Evil is that to which your faith prompts you, should you be faithful!" (Quran 2:93)

However, in verse 2:96, God likens the Jews who refused to obey Moses to *mushrikin*:

And you will most certainly find them the greediest of men for life (greedier) than even those who are polytheists. (Quran 2:96)

The phrase "Those who are polytheists" is a direct translation of the Arabic sentence *mina al-ladhina ashraku* clearly distinguishing between *mushrikin* and this Jewish sect. This is not to say that Islam endorses what it disagrees with in Jewish doctrine, but it does make a legal distinction between the two, thus laying out a different set of rules than those laid out for pagans and idols worshippers.

The Quran repeatedly calls upon the People of the Book to revert to their revealed scriptures and to adhere to their true teachings and instructs Muslims to form an agreement with them to only worship the one God. It further instructs Muslims to debate politely and kindly with the People of the Book and treat them with the utmost respect: "And argue not with the People of the Book unless it be in (a way) that is in kindness" (Quran 29:46). The verse continues by emphasizing the importance of the common foundation that God wants everyone to adhere to—which is surrender to His will and abide by His revelations to His messengers: "And say: We believe in that which hath been revealed unto us and revealed unto you; our Allah and your Allah is One, and unto Him we surrender" (Quran 29:46).

Being unjustly attacked by People of the Book or by other Muslims

The Quran, as explained above, warns the People of the Book not to adopt doctrine that renders them polytheists and warns of punishment in the hereafter for doing so. It further gives permission to Muslims to fight back *if* they are unjustly attacked by the People of The Book. However, this permission is also given to Muslims if one Muslim party transgresses against another Muslim party. The rule for engaging a transgressor is clearly laid out in the following verse:

> If two groups of the faithful fight one another, make peace between them. But if one party of them aggresses against the other, fight the one which aggresses until it returns to Allah's ordinance. Then, if it returns, make peace between them fairly, and do justice. Indeed Allah loves the just. (Quran 49:9)

Defending both Muslims and the People of the Book

Furthermore, Muslims are required to come to the aid of a party of the People of Book if aggression has been levied against them. Ayatullah Sayyid Muhammad Hussain Fadl-Allah issued the following verdict which makes it obligatory upon Muslims to come to the aid of any party that is transgressed against, regardless of whether it is Muslim or not: "Defensive jihad does not stop at defending oneself, property, honor, etc., rather it goes far beyond this circle to cover the defense of others, be they Muslim or non-Muslim."[39]

How the Quran says to treat polytheists

Many Western writers who are critical of Islam are quick to reference verses from the Quran that deal with polytheists and cite them as

39. Fatwas by Ayatullah Fadl-Allah, section 10, page 1

evidence for how Islam legitimizes war against Christianity and Judaism. These same verses are used by Muslim extremist leaders to instigate hate and legitimize terrorist activities against the West.

Yet, when we examine the Quran's verses that deal with polytheists, we find stark differences between how the two groups are to be dealt with.

The verses that deal with idol worshippers instruct Muslims to be fair but not tolerant of their polytheism. Tolerance with misinterpreting God's rightly sent messages to the Jews and Christians is vastly different from tolerating polytheism, which is in direct violation of the essence of all of God's messages—that is, the oneness and unity of God.

Chapter nine of the Quran refers to *mushrikin* and sets the rules for dealing with those among them who inhabited Mecca. The term *mushrikin* is used to describe idolaters without qualification, and Muslims are instructed to prevent all idol worshippers from entering Mecca.

The Quran rejects the notion that an alliance can be forged with polytheists on the basis that they do not adhere to the one God; therefore, they cannot be trusted to obey His commands: "How shall the polytheists have any [valid] treaty with Allah and His Apostle?! (Barring those with whom you made a treaty at the Holy Mosque; so long as they are steadfast with you, be steadfast with them. Indeed Allah loves the Godwary.)" (Quran 9:7)

Misinterpretations of Verses

Terrorists and anti-Muslim writers alike cite verses, including the so-called "verse of the sword,"[40] out of context to prove that Islam calls for killing all those who oppose it. Writers often refer to anyone who opposes Islam as *kafir* which literally translates into 'nonbeliever' but choose to use the English word 'infidel' instead of 'nonbeliever'

---

40. Quran 4:89

as the translation. Both the Arabic word *kafir* and the English 'infidel' have extremely negative connotations and are designed to render one who opposes the belief system a heathen.

A fair, scholarly investigation of the verses they use reveals that the verses specifically deal with tactical war issues and are not guidelines for dealing with all those who oppose Islam.

The true foundation for engaging non-Muslims is that "there is no compulsion in religion" (Quran 2:256). However, Muslims must come to the realization that not all Muslim governments and groups have adhered to this significant rule throughout the centuries. There are those among Muslims who employ Quranic verses out of context to achieve political or other gains causing significant damage to their enemies and Islam equally. It is notable that these groups inflict heinous crimes against Muslims and non-Muslims alike with their erroneous interpretation of the Quran. They do so by first declaring Muslim groups who oppose them heretics—in direct violation of Prophet Muhammad's declaration that anyone who believes that there is only one God is protected under Islamic law.

We have discussed how the Quran makes a clear distinction between Jews and Christians on one hand and idol worshippers on the other. Nevertheless, there are those Muslims who, due to intentional or unintentional misinterpretation of the Quran, treat the People of the Book as idolaters, which is in direct violation of Islam's teachings.

What Shia Islam Teaches About War

Shia scholars, in general, make clear such a distinction and issue verdicts concerning war that take this understanding of the Quran into account. Ayatullah Nasar Makaram Shirazi, a prominent Shia grand scholar with significant following around the world, summed up the Shia view when he said the following:

There is a clear distinction between a Christian and a polytheist from Islam's point of view; Islam has never accepted that a polytheist is a Muslim for two reasons:

A polytheist rejects the principle of prophethood, which is the second principle after acknowledging the existence of Almighty Allah according to all divine religions. Because polytheists do not acknowledge this important principle, it becomes impossible for them to accept the divine teachings and guidance that lead to salvation in the hereafter. For the possibilities of accepting Islam are found in those who believe in the principle of prophethood and who gradually start to be guided to this religion through this belief.

The polytheism of the idolatrous is clear as opposed to the polytheism of (Trinitarian) Christianity which is a weaker state than the former. For even the Trinitarians speak of the oneness of God and say that the trinity does not violate it (even though there is a clear contradiction in their statement). Therefore, a Muslim man may marry a Christian woman but may not marry a polytheist one. (weekly fatwas taken from his website)

Shaykh Dr. Ahmad Waeli, a prolific speaker and renowned authority on history and Islamic law, and a graduate of both Shia and Sunni schools, gave an important lecture twenty years earlier highlighting the difference between the People of The Book and *mushrikin* in the Islamic legal system. Dr. Waeli stated that the main reason Islamic laws treat the People of the Book with much more respect is because they are recipients of divine revelations that regulate their conduct according to moral and ethical teachings that largely comply with Islam's own teachings. Therefore, it is expected that they would positively contribute to a virtuous society while polytheists would not be expected to have the same level of moral and ethical contribution. He further stated that because the People of the Book adhere to revelations, it is expected that they would abide by treaties and agreements that are struck between them and Muslims.[41] Most Shia scholars tend to cite the reasoning employed by Ayatullah Shirazi as monotheism is of paramount importance to Islam.

What Salafi Islam Teaches About War

Conversely, scholars from other Muslim schools of thought make very little or no distinction between *mushrikin* and the People of the Book. The Salafi sect is chief among these schools of thought that employ such strict judgements against all those who oppose its understanding of Islam and calls them polytheists. The Salafi sect is also known as the Wahhabi sect in reference to Muhammad ibn Abd al-Wahhab, their eighteenth century leader.

Followers of this sect deem all others, including Muslims whom they oppose, polytheists and, therefore, legitimate targets of war. Using this justification, Salafi terrorists in Iraq continue to target Shias and, in many cases, Sunnis with their suicide bombs. They also rely on this same understanding to carry out their attacks in the West including the September 11 attacks on New York City and subsequent operations in England and Spain.

Terrorism in Islamic Terminology

The term 'terrorism' as it relates to the Middle East was first coined by Israel in describing Palestinian insurgents. In the West, this term carries with it an extremely negative connotation as it is derived from the word 'terror.' In the Middle East, however, the Arabic word that is used to label those whom the West calls "terrorists" is *mukharibin*.

41. a lecture in Muharram in the Persian Gulf in 1985

When the term 'terrorists' started to be used by Israel, most Arabs viewed it as a disingenuous description of people who were fighting to liberate their homeland. It was incomprehensible to see how the Palestinians would seek to create mischief in their land, as the word *mukharibin* means 'those who seek to create mischief' and not 'terrorists.' In fact, the word *mukharibin* is often used to describe mischievous children and not dangerous terrorists.

Yet over time, the word used to describe terrorists was changed to *irhabeain* which means 'those who create fear,' and the term came to be associated with America's war on those who militarily oppose its policies in the Middle East. Muslims no longer viewed the term *irhabeain* as a disingenuous attempt to describe innocently displaced Palestinians but rather as an attempt to either falsely accuse freedom fighters of creating terror or as an accurate description of criminals who kill in the name of Islam, depending on individual Muslim interpretations of current events.

The term 'terrorist' became an American political term and came to have deep implications in the Middle Eastern Muslim psyche. Anyone who is labeled a terrorist is now viewed as fighting America whether his fight is just or not. Therefore, using such term without understanding its implications on the individual conflict can be dangerous.

After the fall of Saddam Hussein, the newly elected Iraqi government asked me to recommend some methods of ideologically countering the powerful Arab media that painted all Iraqi insurgents as freedom fighters. One of my recommendations was that *The Iraqia*, Iraq's official television station, should stop using the word *irhabeain* and start using the Muslim word *khawarij*, which refers to rebels who fought against early Muslims shortly after the death of Prophet Muhammad. I suggested that the Iraqis stop using the word *irhabeain* because, although it carries a bad meaning, it denotes those who fight America, thus giving a sense of legitimacy to their actions in the minds of many Muslims who oppose America's presence in Iraq.

The word *khawarij*, on the other hand, conjures up memories of rebels who were known to have killed innocent Muslims after the dawn of Islam simply because they disagreed with the *Khawarij's* strict and literal interpretation of the Quran.

Terrorism According to Shia Islam

The Quran has no tolerance for terrorism and sets forth harsh punishment for those who perpetrate it. Quranic verse 5:33 defines terrorists as those who create mischief and fear in the land and applies the hardest punishment in Islam's penal code—capital punishment or complete exile from the land. Some scholars interpret exile as imprisonment. This form of capital punishment is not found anywhere else in the Quran or teachings of Islam because terrorism is a crime not just against an individual but against a whole society, and it often spans the taking of lives and destruction of property—both having great sanctity in the faith.

Islam places a great deal of importance on defending one's land and freedom to worship as we have discussed. Therefore, liberation movements that come into existence with this sole purpose are encouraged in accordance with Islam's instructions. The greatest challenge for Muslim jurists lies not in issuing verdicts that deem terrorism prohibited in Islam but in trusting the West's labeling of any Muslim movement that takes up arms (with the declared intention of liberating its land) as 'terrorism.'

The customary process by which a grand scholar derives and issues a verdict is first understanding the issue at hand, then identifying which canon applies to the situation, and, finally, discerning the elements within the situation and how the canon applies to those elements. But since many Muslims mistrust the motives and long-term plans of Western powers, taking Western labels of individuals and movements at face value violates the guidelines of how scholars should rule on matters. This has been especially true since the onset of colonialism and the post-Ottoman Empire era when Muslims saw their lands come under the grip of one wave of occupation after another with relentless attempts to control the wealth and resources of Muslim lands.

This is not a political matter but an issue of adhering to one's faith, according to Shia scholars. Having stated the above, Shia scholars were very quick to condemn the crimes perpetrated against America on September 11, 2001—not for any political gain, but because they genuinely understood those crimes as having violated Islam's core teachings.

The September 11 attacks, according to Shia scholars, contradicted Prophet Muhammad's instruction to Muslim armies not to attack anyone "who is tilling his field." He said this when fighting back was first legislated in Islam as polytheists were preparing to overtake Medina, the early Muslim stronghold. After much insistence by the Muslims to Prophet Muhammad to allow them to fight back, God's revelation was sent to Muslims, through Prophet Muhammad, giving permission for Muslims to fight back. Upon receiving these verses, Prophet Muhammad issued a declaration outlining the guidelines for engaging in war. Part of this declaration reads as follows:

> March in the name of Allah, by Allah, and on the path of the messenger of Allah, and do not kill an old man, or a child, or a youngster, or a woman, . . . do not cut down a tree, do not interfere with one who is tilling his field.[42]

The statement "Do not interfere with one who is tilling his field" is understood by Shia scholars to mean those who are engaged in their daily work. The World Trade Center was bustling with those who were "tilling their fields" mindless of any war between the American

---

42. Sunan Ibi Daoud. 104:2624. p. 2616, n.d.

government and any group. Therefore, according to Shias, attacking them was in direct violation of the teachings of Prophet Muhammad.

Another aspect of the September 11 attacks that violated Islam's teachings is that they came without warning. It may appear unreasonable to some that Muslims should warn their enemies of impending attacks, but one must understand that Islam preaches the preservation of life as the holiest of God's trusts to humankind.

In the encyclopedia, Wasaʾelu Shia, which is used as the foundation of traditions by all Shia scholars to derive verdicts, Prophet Muhammad instructs the Muslims to attempt to engage in war, if they must, in early afternoons, as "it allows those of the enemy soldiers who flee to get away." He clearly wished that their lives be spared. Likewise, Muslims must first attempt to solve any dispute with negotiations and, if that fails, by repeated warnings. They must only resort to martial means if all other methods fail. Shia scholars have consensus in this regard.

Ayatullah Khomeini ruled that, in regard to defense, it is an obligatory precaution to start with the least harmful method, escalate to warnings, then threats, and finally to the least harmful weapons. Using lethal weapons can only be used as a last resort.[43]

The former president of Iran and Shia scholar, Sayyid Muhammad Khatami, was the first world leader to condemn the events of Sept. 11, followed by Ayatullah Muhammad Hussain Fadl-Allah of Lebanon. Both Khatami and Fadl-Allah cited the violation of Islamic teachings of those attacks in their condemnations.

It is notable that almost every instance of Muslim condemnation of the September 11 events was followed by a call to eradicate the roots of terrorism. For example, in an interview by CNN conducted on December 12, 2001, President Khatami said the following:

---

43. *Tahrir al-Wasilah*, defense fatwa 6.

> What kind of anger was created that must have been expressed
> in that way? So, no doubt there must have been some wrong
> policies that created a kind of hatred that became extreme.
> The people of America should demand [that their government]
> moderate its policies to improve and change some of it. And
> if that happens the situation in the world will also improve.

Demanding that condemnation of terrorism be associated with a call
for understanding the causes that lead to such acts is a reflection of
how Muslim scholarly thought manifests itself. In both Shia and Sunni
schools of thought, a scholar must give evidence from the Quran, or
other acceptable sources of legislation, to support his ruling, and he
must allow the opposing perspectives to be accommodated. Therefore,
one should understand that while Muslim scholars consider terrorism
an evil to be eradicated, they consider the root causes of terrorism
more evil (e.g., Khatami's CNN interview). There is always an implied,
or even explicit, allegation that the actions of the West, in general,
and the United States of America, specifically, contribute to the events
that led to such acts of terror. From a Muslim scholar's perspective,
maintaining this religious equilibrium when issuing rulings regarding
any subject, including terrorism, is the only method to avoid the label
of hypocrisy, which is among the worst of labels given by Islam to
any category of people.

Shia Verdicts Dealing With the Realities of Post September 11

Reacting to a number of issues that have arisen after the tragic
events of September 11, a number of Shia scholars issued verdicts
and declarations to their followers, especially those in the West,
that prepare them to deal with the aftermath of those events and to
educate them on their duties toward their newly found communities.

Ayatullah Muhammad Hussain Fadl-Allah declared that a visa granted by any government to an immigrant or visitor to that country constitutes a legally binding contract that must be observed according to Islam's teachings, and, therefore, Muslims must obey all of the laws of the host country. Ayatullah Khamenei, the supreme leader of the Islamic Republic of Iran, issued a similar verdict and called on his followers to act as model citizens of their countries wherever they are.

When Ayatullah Khamenei issued a verdict declaring the possession of nuclear weapons prohibited according to the teachings of Islam, many in the Shia world expected this verdict to lessen the fears of Western governments that Iran intends to develop such weapons. The verdict, ultimately, according to Shia public psyche, made it clear that developing such weapons is in violation of Islam's laws and, thus, the debate should have been over. However, because the West does not have the same understanding of how these verdicts are viewed and respected, the news of the verdict went unnoticed by Western media.

Notwithstanding the disregard for Khamenei's verdict, Islam clearly prohibits the use of nuclear weapons under all circumstances. Prophet Muhammad's declaration at Medina gives precise details of how the innocent and their properties should not be harmed in a war: poison and chemical weapons are prohibited according to Islamic teachings because they are considered indiscriminate weapons (i.e., they cannot distinguish between the innocent and the combatant), and the use of fire on enemy lands is regulated such that vegetation must not be harmed. These restrictions render the prohibition of the use of nuclear weapons obvious under Islamic law.

However, one can argue that the possession of such weapons for deterrent purposes, without the intent to actually deploy them, is a different matter according to Islamic law. The Quran calls upon Muslims to prepare their armies and equip them with all the means needed to create fear in their enemies. As seen above, Islam does not teach its soldiers that the purpose of battle is to kill the enemy's soldiers but rather to force them either to capitulate or to get away from the battlefield without harming Muslim soldiers. Quranic verses 8:60–61 undoubtedly show that the purpose for engaging in war is not to kill or destroy the enemy but rather to compel it to accept peace:

> Prepare against them whatever you can of [military] power and war-horses, awing thereby the enemy of Allah, and your enemy, and others besides them, whom you do not know, but Allah knows them. And whatever you spend in the way of Allah will be repaid to you in full, and you will not be wronged. And if they incline toward peace, then you [too] incline toward it, and put your trust in Allah. Indeed He is the All-hearing, the All-knowing. (Quran 8:60–61)

These verses, combined with Prophet Muhammad's instructions to his followers not to throw poison in the lands of the enemy or cut trees or kill the innocent, show that the purpose of entering the battlefield or possessing fearful weapons is not to create destruction but to establish peace. In other words, the purpose of the existence of Muslim armies and equipping them with powerful weapons, including nuclear ones, it can be argued, is for deterrence only.

This thinking is commonplace in Shia schools of thought, and the government of Iran would be hard-pressed not to comply with such deduction. However, Khamenei's verdict, which prohibits the possession and use of nuclear weapons, renders ineffectual this seemingly reasonable justification of owning nuclear weapons for defensive purposes.

Chapter Eight

Parallels in Shia Islam and Catholicism

Although the formation of what became iconic beliefs in Catholicism took a different historical path than that of Shia Islam, the mere existence of these concepts in Shia Islam is striking. The Catholic beliefs in the sanctity of saints, the papacy, intercession, purgatory, and prayers for the dead share similarities with Shia Islam. While many of such beliefs appear to have developed over time in Catholicism, the entire set of Shia beliefs can verifiably be traced back to the Prophet's first righteous heir, Imam Ali ibn Abi Talib (the first of the twelve princes mentioned in Genesis 17:20).

The Need for an Heir

Simon Peter is appointed heir

A foundational event in both faiths was the assignment of an heir by the patriarchs Jesus and Muhammad. Saint Simon Peter, known as "Simon the Pure" or Simon al-Safa in Islamic literature, is a key figure in Catholicism. He is said to hold the "keys to the Church" and is the rock on which Jesus' teachings will continue to exist.

Simon Peter holds the first place in the college of the Twelve; Jesus entrusted a unique mission to him. Through a revelation from the Father, Peter had confessed: "You are the Christ, the Son of the living God." Our Lord then declared to him: "You are Peter, and on this rock I will build my Church, and the gates of Hades will not prevail against it." Christ, the "living stone, "thus assures his Church, built on Peter, of victory over the powers of death. Because of the faith he confessed, Peter will remain the unshakeable rock of the Church. His mission will be to keep this faith from every lapse and to strengthen his brothers in it.

Jesus entrusted a specific authority to Peter: "I will give you the keys of the kingdom of heaven, and whatever you bind on earth shall be bound in heaven, and whatever you loose on earth shall be loosed in heaven. "The "power of the keys" designates authority to govern the house of God, which is the Church. Jesus, the Good Shepherd, confirmed this mandate after his Resurrection: "Feed my sheep. "The power to "bind and loose" connotes the authority to absolve sins, to pronounce doctrinal judgments, and to make disciplinary decisions in the Church. Jesus entrusted this authority to the Church through the ministry of the apostles and in particular through the ministry of Peter, the only one to whom he specifically entrusted the keys of the kingdom.[44]

This means that Jesus appointed Simon Peter as the leader of the church after Jesus. Jesus also disclosed to Simon Peter the suffering he, Simon Peter, would endure for being vested in this role. After Jesus' declaration of Simon Peter as the "rock of the Church" and entrusting him with Christianity, Jesus began preparing for his

---

44. US Catholic Conference, *Catechism of the Catholic Church,* Continuum International, 2000.

departure from this lower world. Jesus departed shortly thereafter and left Simon Peter to lead his flocks.

The teachings of Shia Islam also assert Simon Peter to be the righteous heir of Jesus. Islam agrees that Simon Peter was entrusted by him with the "keys" and was given complete authority to govern the "house of God." The reference to the "house of God" is understood to be all of God's creation, or the Temple of Jerusalem.

Imam Ali is appointed heir

The accounts of succession of both Jesus Christ and Prophet Muhammad are parallel in narrative. The teachings of Shia Islam assert that the first heir (*imam*) to Prophet Muhammad was Imam Ali. Imam Ali was approached by Prophet Muhammad and told that he was to be the "gate to the city of knowledge." The "city of knowledge" in this case referred to the Prophet himself.

Similarly, Simon Peter was given the "keys to the Church" by Jesus. The keys are the set of teachings from Jesus Christ. As the faithful must come to Jesus through Simon Peter after Jesus' departure, so must the faithful come to Muhammad through Ali after Prophet Muhammad's departure from this world. Prophet Muhammad informs Imam Ali that he, Imam Ali, will suffer at the hands of the same people who profess his faith for Imam Ali being vested as *imam*.

Prophet Muhammad prepared for his own death by gathering all of the companions who had joined him on his final pilgrimage to Mecca. In this event, called Ghadir Khumm, he announced that his death was near and that Ali would be his official righteous heir, a fact Prophet Muhammad had stated on a number of preceding occasions.

The event of Ghadir Khumm is paramount in the history of Shia Islam. A revelation from God came to Prophet Muhammad:

O Apostle! Deliver what has been sent down to you from your Lord; and if you don't do it, you have not delivered His message (at all); and God will protect you from the people.[45]

Prophet Muhammad gathered the one-hundred-thousand-strong procession who accompanied him on his journey back from his last pilgrimage to Mecca to deliver a speech:

It seems the time approached when I shall be called away (by God) and I shall answer that call. I am leaving for you two precious things and if you adhere to them both, you will never go astray after me. They are the Book of God and my Progeny that is my Ahlul Bayt. The two shall never separate from each other until they come to me by the Pool (of Paradise). Do I not have more right over the believers than what they have over themselves?[46]

When the people responded with "Yes, O' Messenger of God," Prophet Muhammad held up the hand of Ali and made the statement that denotes the clear designation of Ali as the first leader of the Muslims: "For whoever I am his Leader (*mawla*), Ali is his Leader (*mawla*)." He then continued, "O' God, love those who love him, and be hostile to those who are hostile to him."[47]

Immediately following the completion of Prophet Muhammad's speech, a new verse of the Quran was revealed: "Today I have perfected your religion for you, and I have completed My blessing upon you, and I have approved Islam as your religion" (Quran 5:3).

45. *Event of Ghadir Khumm,* Ahl Bayt Digital Islamic Library Project, accessed 2015, http://www.al-Islam.org/ghadir/incident.htm.
46. Ibid.
47. Ibid.

This verse is understood by Shia Muslims to indicate that without clearing up the matter of who holds the succession after Prophet Muhammad, Islam was not complete. The completion of religion was owed to the assignment of the Prophet's immediate successor. Prophet Muhammad's choice of words, believed to be divinely revealed, indicates that the presence of the Quran alone is insufficient. This is further proven in Prophet Muhammad's statement "I am leaving for you two precious things and if you adhere to them both, you will never go astray after me. They are the Book of God and my Progeny that is my Ahl al-Bayt."

Simon Peter appears to Imam Ali

Shia narrations contain myriad statements about Jesus—things he said and did and record of what law was revealed to him by God. These narrations do not come from any Christian source. They come directly from the present knowledge of Prophet Muhammad and his twelve successors. Having present knowledge means one was not taught by another person—the knowledge comes from God. (As we discussed before, that's why it's so important to know if the Prophet or an *imam* really did say what they are said to have said—if they really did say it, we can take it as God's will and truth.)

In a narration, Simon Peter is said to have appeared to Imam Ali near a mountain at Siffin at the time for evening prayers to console him (because they both struggled against people who questioned their authority and wanted to destroy the messages they were tasked with preserving). Imam Ali said to his companions around him who had heard Simon Peter, "He is Simon, the successor of Jesus (a). Allah sent him to me to give me solace for this confrontation with His enemies."[48]

Imam Ali has a special connection to Jesus as well. Narrations say that Imam Ali died on the same day in the lunar calendar that Jesus was raised.

---

48. Qaim, *Jesus through Shiite Narrations,* accessed January 2016.

On the night of the twenty-first, Jesus (a) was raised and the executor of Moses was taken in it, and the Commander of the Faithful [Imam Ali] was taken in it.[49]

When the Commander of the Faithful [Imam Ali] passed away, Hasan (a) stood and spoke. He said, "O you people! On this night Jesus the son of Mary was raised."[50]

Believers need both scripture and a leader

Prophet Muhammad said Muslims need both their book of guidance (the Quran) and his Ahl al-Bayt (the twelve imams who came after him) in order to never go astray.

Catholicism teaches something similar. The Holy See's website says, "In order that the full and living Gospel might always be preserved in the Church the apostles left bishops as their successors. They gave them their own position of teaching authority. Indeed, 'the apostolic preaching, which is expressed in a special way in the inspired books, was to be preserved in a continuous line of succession until the end of time.'"[51]

The Doctrine of Infallibility

Infallibility in the Roman Catholic Church

The Holy See says Christ conferred on the church a share of his own infallibility. It is the task of the Pope and bishops to guarantee God's people receive a faith without error. Christ endowed them with infallibility in matters of faith and morals.

---

49. Ibid.
50. Ibid.
51. The Holy See, "Catechism of the Catholic Church," accessed 2016, http://www.vatican.va/archive/ccc_css/archive/catechism/p1s1c2a2.htm.

In order to preserve the Church in the purity of the faith handed on by the apostles, Christ who is the Truth willed to confer on her a share in his own infallibility. By a "supernatural sense of faith" the People of God, under the guidance of the Church's living Magisterium, "unfailingly adheres to this faith."

The mission of the Magisterium is linked to the definitive nature of the covenant established by God with his people in Christ. It is this Magisterium's task to preserve God's people from deviations and defections and to guarantee them the objective possibility of professing the true faith without error. Thus, the pastoral duty of the Magisterium is aimed at seeing to it that the People of God abides in the truth that liberates. To fulfill this service, Christ endowed the Church's shepherds with the charism of infallibility in matters of faith and morals. The exercise of this charism takes several forms:

The Roman Pontiff, head of the college of bishops, enjoys this infallibility in virtue of his office, when, as supreme pastor and teacher of all the faithful - who confirms his brethren in the faith he proclaims by a definitive act a doctrine pertaining to faith or morals . . . The infallibility promised to the Church is also present in the body of bishops when, together with Peter's successor, they exercise the supreme Magisterium," above all in an Ecumenical Council. When the Church through its supreme Magisterium proposes a doctrine "for belief as being divinely revealed," and as the teaching of Christ, the definitions "must be adhered to with the obedience of faith." This infallibility extends as far as the deposit of divine Revelation itself.[52]

---

52. The Holy See, "Catechism of the Catholic Church," accessed 2016, http://www.vatican.va/archive/ccc_css/archive/catechism/p123a9p4.htm.

Infallibility in Shia Islam

All Muslims agree that the prophets, including Prophet Muhammad, were infallible. However, Muslims differ in the degree of infallibility the prophets had. The majority of Muslim schools of thought believe in the full infallibility of Prophet Muhammad. They believe that 1) since Islam is a complete way of life and 2) since there is not an action or dimension in an individual's life that they are not accountable for and 3) since Prophet Muhammad was a guiding light in all that he did, he must have been infallible in everything he said and did. A minority view is that the Prophet need only have been infallible in matters relating to the delivery of the revealed message.

The doctrine of infallibility according to Shia Islam is based on the logical argument that since God is just, He will send humanity a way to distinguish between good and evil. Since God willed that humans have free will with the right to choose between good and evil, God will judge us based on our choices. Therefore, a just God will send a message distinguishing between the good choices and the bad ones.

> We said, "Get down from it, all together! Yet, should any guidance come to you from Me, those who follow My guidance shall have no fear, nor shall they grieve." (Quran 2:38)

God would not be just if He judged us based on an error-ridden message. Given that God commands us to obey the prophets without distinction[53] and calls the message delivered to people "God's guidance," it becomes inconceivable that the prophets themselves would err in delivering the infallible message.

---

53. The Apostle has faith in what has been sent down to him from his Lord, and all the faithful. Each [of them] has faith in Allah, His angels, His scriptures and His apostles. [They declare,] "We make no distinction between any of His apostles." And they say, "We hear and obey. Our Lord, forgive us, and toward You is the return." (Quran 2:285)

The Quran emphasizes the infallibility of Prophet Muhammad, including his words, in the following verses:

> your companion [That is, the Apostle of Allah] has neither gone astray, nor gone amiss. Nor does he speak out of [his own] desire: it is just a revelation that is revealed [to him], taught him by One of great powers, possessed of sound judgement (Quran 53:2-6)

Those who reject this doctrine argue that if a prophet is infallible, then he must be obeyed unconditionally. Doing so would lead to a form of polytheism. However, we understand that these infallible prophets are chosen directly by God. Obedience to these infallible people stems from obeying God's command to follow them. In other words, to obey Abraham, Moses, Jesus, and Muhammad because God commanded it is not in defiance of worshipping Him alone. The Quran clearly instructs the unconditional submittal to Prophet Muhammad:

> Take whatever the Apostle gives you, and relinquish whatever he forbids you. (Quran 59:7)
>
> Say, "Obey Allah and the Apostle." But if they turn away, indeed Allah does not like the faithless. (Quran 3:32)

Infallibility in those who carry on the message

Not only must the message and the messenger be infallible to comply with God's attribute of justice, but the continuation of the message to future generations must also be guaranteed through infallibility. This appears to be the root of the Catholic doctrine of infallibility as well.

The Quran makes clear that the role of human vicegerency on Earth is to glorify Him in praise, which is the ultimate form of worship—God's stated purpose of creating humankind. Since human beings are not omniscient, they are prone to err in worshipping God as He deserves to be worshipped. For this reason, God chooses at least one infallible human being in each time period, from Adam to when the heavens and Earth pass away, to worship Him as He deserves and to continue to remind us of His message, even in the absence of prophets and messengers. Simon Peter was such a person, and Imam Ali (the appointed heir after Prophet Muhammad) was such a person. Simon Peter would have appointed such a person (chosen by God) before he died, and Imam Ali appointed such a person (chosen by God) before he died.

Intercession

It is notable that the centers of authority of both faiths are located in and around the shrines of the first of the twelve disciples of the patriarchs of the faiths. Simon Peter's shrine is the center of the Vatican, and Imam Ali's is the center of Najaf, Iraq. Catholics revere whom they call saints, and Shia Muslims revere whom they call imams. Both groups erect beautiful shrines for them and regularly visit their sites for prayer and blessings.

Basic Islamic teachings agree that Jesus had God's covenant and, therefore, the power to intercede, as does Muhammad and all other prophets: "Intercession will not avail that day except from him whom the All-beneficent allows and approves of his word" (Quran 20:109).

Upon thorough examination of the belief that Jesus and Muhammad, and saints and imams, intercede on behalf of believers with God, it appears that this belief is identical in both faiths. Shia Muslims, and Muslims in general, consider Jesus a chief interceder on behalf of all believers, including Muslims themselves. The Quran states, "No one will have the power to intercede [with Allah], except for him who has taken a covenant with the All-beneficent" (Quran 19:87).

In Catholic teachings, Jesus intercedes for believers:

Intercession is a prayer of petition which leads us to pray as Jesus did. He is the one intercessor with the Father on behalf of all men, especially sinners. He is "able for all time to save those who draw near to God through him, since he always lives to make intercession for them." The Holy Spirit "himself intercedes for us...and intercedes for the saints according to the will of God."

Since Abraham, intercession—asking on behalf of another—has been characteristic of a heart attuned to God's mercy. In the age of the Church, Christian intercession participates in Christ's, as an expression of the communion of saints. In intercession, he who prays looks "not only to his own interests, but also to the interests of others," even to the point of praying for those who do him harm.[54]

Intercession is the absolute right of God to extend to whom He wills. He may choose to extend it to certain people among His creation. The Quran states:

There is no intercessor, except by His leave. That is Allah, your Lord! So worship Him. (Quran 10:3)

Who is it that may intercede with Him except with His permission? (Quran 2:255)

Intercession will not avail that day except from him whom the All-beneficent allows and approves of his word. (Quran 20:109)

And they do not intercede except for someone He approves of, and they are apprehensive for the fear of Him. (Quran 21:28)

---

54. The Holy See, "Catechism of the Catholic Church," accessed 2016, http://www.vatican.va/archive/ccc_css/archive/catechism/p4s1c1a3.htm.

No one will have the power to intercede [with Allah], except for him who has taken a covenant with the All-beneficent. (Quran 19:87)

According to these verses, certain people will have permission from God, such as prophets, imams, and *awliya* (intimate friends of God) to intercede and help people by the permission of God. Without His permission, no intercession will be accepted. Even during their lifetime, prophets had the ability to intercede on behalf of those who repented and sought forgiveness and returned to the path of God. The Quran states:

We did not send any apostle but to be obeyed by Allah's leave. Had they, when they wronged themselves, come to you and pleaded to Allah for forgiveness, and the Apostle had pleaded for forgiveness for them, they would have surely found Allah all-clement, all-merciful. (Quran 4:64)

They [Joseph's brothers] said, "Father! Plead [with Allah] for forgiveness of our sins! We have indeed been erring." He said, "I shall plead with my Lord to forgive you; indeed He is the All-forgiving, the All-merciful." (Quran 12:97–98)

Prophet Muhammad has also mentioned to the people in regards to his own intercession:

I will be interceding on the Day of Judgement for whoever has faith in his heart. Each prophet before me asked God for something which he was granted, and I saved my request until the Day of Judgement for intercession on behalf of my nation. My intercession will be for the people who committed the cardinal sins (*al-kabair*) except shirk and polytheism and oppression.

> The Intercessors are five: the Quran, one's near relatives, trusts, your Prophet, and the family of your Prophet (the Ahl al-Bayt).[55]

As the Holy Quran asserts, only those who receive a covenant and permission from God may intercede and help people on the Day of Judgement. Intercession will be for those with good intentions and good belief in this life, who neither defied God nor challenged His authority but perhaps fell behind in part of their religious obligations. Their good record will help them receive the intercession of the messengers, the imams, and the believers on the Day of Judgement.

Purgatory

Catholics and Shia Muslims, and, indeed, most Muslims, believe in a state that our spirits move to after death and prior to resurrection. While it appears that Catholics believe purgatory to be strictly a stage of purification for those who had fallen short of full salvation (where the believers may suffer some torment as a measure of purification before entering heaven), Muslims believe that all humans encounter the stage of purgatory (*barzakh*).

According to Catholic teachings, "All who die in God's grace and friendship, but still imperfectly purified, are indeed assured of their eternal salvation; but after death they undergo purification, so as to achieve the holiness necessary to enter the joy of heaven."[56]

In describing the torment which Pharaoh and his clan encounter in *barzakh*, the Quran states, "the Fire, to which they are exposed morning and evening. And on the day when the Hour sets in Pharaoh's clan

---

55. Al-Khazini, *Mizan al-Hikamah,* vol. 1. p. 404, 1121 CE.
56. The Holy See, "Catechism of the Catholic Church," accessed 2016, http://www.vatican.va/archive/ccc_css/archive/catechism/p123a12.htm.

will enter the severest punishment" (Quran 40:46). The twelfth imam, Imam Mahdi, was asked to explain the meaning of the Quranic verse "And ahead of them is a barrier until the day they will be resurrected" (23:100). His response was that "It's the grave, in it there is stressful torment for them in it. By God, the grave is surely either a garden of the gardens of heaven or a pit of the pits of the Hell fire."[57] Imam Sadiq, the sixth imam of Shia Muslims said, "By God I only fear for you during barzakh."[58] Imam Sadiq meant that believers ultimately enter heaven eternally, but he fears for them the torment in *barzakh,* which is seen as a purification before resurrection.

Praying for the Dead

While some Muslim sects reject the practice of praying for the dead, Shia and most Sunni schools believe in and encourage this practice. Catholic teachings are consistent with those of Islam in this manner.

This teaching is also based on the practice of prayer for the dead, already mentioned in Sacred Scripture: "Therefore [Judas Maccabeus] made atonement for the dead, that they might be delivered from their sin." From the beginning the Church has honored the memory of the dead and offered prayers in suffrage for them, above all the Eucharistic sacrifice, so that, thus purified, they may attain the beatific vision of God. The Church also commends almsgiving, indulgences, and works of penance undertaken on behalf of the dead:

Let us help and commemorate them. If Job's sons were purified by their father's sacrifice, why would we doubt that our offerings for the dead bring them some consolation? Let us

---

57. Al-Khazini, *Mizan al-Hikamah,* 1121 CE.
58. Ibid.

not hesitate to help those who have died and to offer our prayers for them.[59]

Muslims in general believe in the validity of and goodness of praying for the dead. A common prayer Muslims recite at funerals depicts this belief:

O God, forgive and have mercy upon him, excuse him and pardon him, and make honorable his reception. Expand his entry, and cleanse him with water, snow, and ice, and purify him of sin as a white robe is purified of filth. Exchange his home for a better home, and his family for a better family, and his spouse for a better spouse. Admit him into the garden, protect him from the punishment of the grave and the torment of the fire.

O God, (the name of the deceased is mentioned here) is under your care and protection so protect him from the trial of the grave and torment of the fire. Indeed you are faithful and truthful. Forgive and have mercy upon him, surely you are the oft-forgiving, the most-merciful.

O God, your servant and the son of your maidservant is in need of your mercy and you are without need of his punishment. If he was righteous then increase his reward and if he was wicked then look over his sins.[60]

Reverence for Mary, the Mother of the Christ

Mary, the daughter of Imran, is a name that brings peace and love to the heart of every Muslim. The Holy Quran speaks of Mary—a woman

---

59. Ali, Saeed bin. n.d. The Muslim's Fastness from Quran & Sunnah.
60. Ibid.

who was elected by Almighty God to give birth to God's spirit, Jesus
the Messiah. Mary is a name so revered among Muslims that many
women are named after her.

In the second chapter of the Quran, Jesus is honorably called "the
son of Mary" (2:87). God tells us how Imran's wife prayed that the
child in her womb would be dedicated to His service. That child was
Mary. Imran's wife also prayed that Mary and her offspring would
be kept safe from Satan. God answered this prayer. When Imran's
wife brought baby Mary to the temple in fulfillment of her promise
to God that the child in her womb would be dedicated to His service,
a dispute occurred between the priests as to who would care for this
holy child. Zechariah, who was the only present prophet, wanted
to protect baby Mary, so he requested that custody of the child be
given to him (3:37).[61]

Mary grew up "pure and beautiful." When Zechariah would see how
Mary was doing at her place of worship (perhaps in the Temple of
Jerusalem as is described in some apocryphal books not in the New
Testament, such as the Gospel of the Nativity of Mary), he would always
find fresh food that was often out of its season. When Zechariah asked
Mary about the food, Mary responded that God had sent her the food
(Quran 3:37). Upon hearing this, Zechariah himself prayed for virtuous
offspring, so God granted him a son, John the Baptist (Quran 3:38–41).

The chapter of the Quran titled "Family of Imran" relates how Mary
was informed by angels that God had purified her and given her
distinction among women. The angels also directed Mary to pray
with devotion to her Lord and bow down in prayer (Quran 3:42–43)
for this lofty position is only given to those who are near to God and
who devote themselves to Him. The angels also told Mary the good
news that she would give birth to a son whom God called "His Word."

---

61. The English translation of the Quran that we reference, the one by Ali Quli
Qarai, says, "He charged Zechariah with her care," but in Arabic, it's clear that
Zechariah volunteered to take care of her.

His name would be Messiah, Jesus the son of Mary. Jesus would be an honorable man, "one of the righteous ones," and be one of the nearest to God. From the cradle, he would speak to people (Quran 3:45–46). The apocryphal Infancy Gospel of Thomas tells of Jesus speaking from the cradle as well, although the character of the child Jesus differs in this apocryphal gospel from the description in the Quran.

Mary, of course, did not understand how she could have a son when she was a chaste virgin. The angels replied that God creates whatever He wants (Quran 3:47). The angels continued by saying that Jesus would be given wisdom by God—God would teach Jesus about the book of Abraham, the Torah, and the Gospel. Mary also learned that Jesus the Messiah would be a messenger of God to the Israelites and that he would show Israel many miracles (Quran 3:48–49).

The events described above in the Quran are similar to, though not identical to, some events described in the first chapter of the Gospel According to Luke, in the apocryphal Gospel of the Nativity of Mary, and in the apocryphal Infancy Gospel Matthew.

The Quran relates that Mary, before delivering her son, withdrew to a distant place. When the labor pains of childbirth began, Mary, with only a palm tree for company, became sad. She declared, "'I wish I had died before this and become a forgotten thing, beyond recall" (19:22–23). But her baby, Jesus, declared to her "Do not grieve," and with those comforting words told her of the stream of water her Lord had just caused to flow at her feet. The infant went on to tell Mary that if she were to shake the trunk of the palm tree, fresh ripe dates would be provided for her. "Eat, drink, and be comforted," exclaimed the baby Jesus to his mother. "Then if you see any human, say, 'Indeed I have vowed a fast to the All-beneficent, so I will not speak to any human today'" (19:24–26).

For this reason, many Muslim women believe it is recommended to eat dates immediately after giving birth to a child. It is also a common Muslim practice for either of the parents to take a very small amount from a date and put it on the newborn baby's tongue before it is given milk for the first time.

Mary then brought the baby Jesus to her people and they said, "O Mary, you have certainly come up with an odd thing! O sister of Aaron['s lineage]! Your father was not an evil man, nor was your mother unchaste." When Mary pointed to the baby, her people responded by saying, "How can we speak to one who is yet a baby in the cradle?" (19:27–29). Then, the baby Jesus declared to the people, "Indeed I am a servant of Allah! He has given me the Book and made me a prophet. He has made me blessed, wherever I may be, and He has enjoined me to [maintain] the prayer and to [pay] the zakat as long as I live, and to be good to my mother, and He has not made me self-willed and wretched. Peace is to me the day I was born, and the day I die, and the day I am raised alive. That is Jesus, son of Mary, a Word of the Real concerning whom they are in doubt" (9:30–34).

In the chapter titled "The Prophets," it states, "And her who guarded her chastity, so We breathed into her Our spirit, and made her and her son a sign for all the nations" (21:91). This passage can be taken as a summary of what the Quran teaches about the Virgin Mary and her son, Jesus the Messiah (peace be upon them both). It is a statement on which both Muslims and Christians agree, and, therefore, the story of the Virgin Mary may be a place for Muslims and Christians to begin friendly dialogue.

Muslim scholars agree that Mary was spoken to by angels. The Quran describes her as Siddiqa, which is one who believes and never tells a lie. The common belief in Sunni Islam is that angels only speak directly to prophets; however, Shia Muslim scholars state that angels speak to prophets and other chosen humans if there is a purpose for such speech. They give the undisputed story of the angel speaking to Mary as proof of their argument.

Conclusion

The Quranic verse quoted at the beginning of this chapter calls on Muslims to believe in all of God's prophets without exception. The verse also states that what the prophets received from their Lord is the same message. Based on this, finding many common beliefs and religious practices between followers of the prophets of God is not surprising. The passage of time, differences in cultural norms, language, and independent development of each faith make these similar beliefs and practices look different. The terminology used, along with modification of the rituals to suit different times and communities are factors that contribute to this seeming differentiation.

Yet, when many of those beliefs and practices are further examined, it becomes apparent they are rooted in the same divine wisdom that God revealed to each of His prophets. The doctrine of the trinity, the belief in the crucifixion of Jesus, and not accepting Muhammad as a prophet of God are major points of disagreement between Christians and Muslims. However, it can be concluded that many other beliefs are in fact the same in form and substance.

Examining these beliefs and practices contributes to the building of bridges between Catholics and Shias, specifically, and between Christians and Muslims in general. The shared examination should lead to unified efforts by both faith communities to help the poor and the destitute and to establish justice and honor.

Summary

S ocial and political competition put Islam and Christianity at odds despite the numerous commonalities they share. No other two faiths share so many fundamental beliefs and moral codes as do these two faiths. Islam and Christianity share the belief that Jesus is the only promised Messiah who is in heaven waiting to come back to establish God's kingdom on Earth.

They both share the belief that he was miraculously born of the chaste Virgin Mary who is the central female figure for the followers of both faiths. Mary is the most common name for Muslim women throughout the 1.6 billion Muslims worldwide. Muslims and Christians also share the Ten Commandments, believe in the miracles of Jesus, and hold that the Holy Spirit was with Jesus since his miraculous birth.

According to USA Today, Islam is the fastest growing religion in the United States and the world. The greatest majority of Muslims are young, and Muslims control over 60% of the world's energy sources. This book is meant to help people develop a better understanding of how Muslims think and to build bridges of peace with them. Muslims share the same Judeo-Christian values that the West espouses. Interpreting the Muslim world solely through politics will lead to a perpetual misunderstanding of a fast-growing and influential segment of humanity. By understanding Muslim beliefs, the West will find much in common, and they will be able to work with Muslims, creating a world of peace and harmony and avoiding an all-out confrontation that would be disastrous to both sides.

◆❖◆

Appendix 1

·············◆◆◆·············

Main Beliefs and
Practices of Shia Muslims

Because the Sunni sects of Islam have more adherents, literature that publicizes Sunni beliefs is more readily found by Westerners looking for information about Islam. Westerners learn that the Sunni sects of Islam can be summarized by five pillars of faith. The five pillars include two beliefs (oneness of God and the prophethood of Muhammad) and four practices (five daily prayers, giving charity, making the pilgrimage to Mecca once in one's lifetime, and fasting during the month of Ramadan). Literature published by the government of Saudi Arabia, which is dominated by the Salafi (Wahhabi) sect, may list "holy war" (the lesser *jihad*) as a sixth pillar, although this is a recent development.

Twelver Shia Muslims (the major Shia sect) present a summary of Islam that is more comprehensive. It has five major beliefs (as opposed to two) and ten major practices (as opposed to four). The summary can visually be thought of as a tree where the trunk of the tree is Islam itself, the roots are the five beliefs, and the branches are the ten practices.

Main Beliefs of Shia Muslims

The first root: Belief in the oneness of God

The first belief is the oneness of God (*tawhid*). There can only be one God (Arabic: *Allah*; Hebrew: *Eloah*; Aramaic: *Allaha*).

Say, "He is Allah, the One. Allah is the All-embracing. He neither begat, nor was begotten, nor has He any equal" (Quran 112:1–4).

God is unique, uncreated, eternal, not born, the Knower (*alim*) of all things, and the Perfect. God cannot be compelled (*murid*). God is true in His words and promises (*sadiq*). God is all-powerful.

To believe in the oneness of God is to accept that God has no partner or partners. God is not composed of any material, nor can He be divided—even in imagination. This concept of God's oneness means that Muslims believe that God cannot be confined to any place or time, does not change, and has no needs. God's attributes cannot be separated from Him.

The second root: Belief in the justice of God

The second root of Islam is the belief that God is just (*adl*). God has promised humanity that He does not wrong anybody. God will not decide at the last minute to send believers to hell and unbelievers to heaven. Each person will be rewarded for even the tiniest amount of good they did—they will be rewarded either in this life or in heaven or in the stage of life between our earthly lives and heaven/hell (the intermediate realm). . .or in one or more of the three places. Any hardship we suffer will be rewarded as well—providing we are patient while experiencing that hardship.

Any actions we take that fall outside of the laws God has laid out for us (a sin) will count against us once we become of age to reason...unless we repent. God is more merciful than anything we can imagine—He's quick to forgive and is waiting for us to turn to Him in repentance.

Islam does not teach that all Muslims will go to heaven and all non-Muslims will go to hell. God will judge people on what they knew and what they did with what they knew, and there's no way any human can know enough about another human to know where they are going on the Day of Judgement (unless God has told us through a prophet). Only God is all-knowing, just, and all-merciful, so we will all be judged perfectly.

Through the Quran and the teachings of Prophet Muhammad and the infallible guides (*imams*) who came after him, we learn that God requires us to act justly as well. There are guidelines for how we should behave justly towards anybody—towards unbelievers, Jews, Christians, rulers, neighbors, relatives, spouses, children, parents, those weaker than us, people who are treating us badly, orphans, widows, travelers, animals, and the environment. We should not let our anger or hatred toward someone cause us to treat them unjustly.

We should also treat ourselves justly—some of the laws that God gives us are so that we treat ourselves justly. Asking God to guide us to act justly is a good prayer.

The third root: Prophecy

God has created the universe to be ruled by calculation and order, from the universe to the atom, for animate beings and non-animate things. He purposively means for humans' lives to be orderly as well. Left to our own devices, we would each do whatever is pleasing to us in order to secure our interests, and the result would be a clash of desires and interests. Individual relationships and social relationships would degenerate to anarchy.

So God has given us innate guidance that is part of our nature and legislative guidance that comes to us through prophets. Prophets acquaint humanity with the codes of life (laws) that, if followed, enable us each to live our best lives without clashes of interest with other people. The needs of individuals, families, and communities are all met in the system by which God means for us to live.

Prophets convey to us divine knowledge, free from all forms of illusion and error. They tell us truths about things we could not have learned unaided because we cannot see them to study them—the effects of our actions on our spirits, death, the intermediate realm, and resurrection. They even teach us truths that humanity, at the time of a given prophet, had not yet discovered scientifically but would in the future.

Prophets teach us balance and moderation. They teach us to tame the actions that cause us torment and harm (even those actions we don't see as causing us harm), and they teach us to reduce the rebelliousness of our spirits so we may approach true happiness. In the spirit of moderation, prophets teach us that pleasures are to be enjoyed in lawful confines, neither excessively practiced nor denied.

All Muslims agree that Adam was the first prophet for humankind. He and the other 124,000 prophets were sent to various peoples at various times in order to provide guidance to the people of that time. Other prophets in whom Muslims believe include Noah, Abraham, Joseph, Moses, David, John the Baptist, Jesus the Messiah, and, of course, Muhammad who was the last prophet (peace be upon them all).

In fundamental principles, the prophets never disagreed. Prophets were sent to different peoples, at different times, in different regions. The last prophet, Muhammad, was sent to all of humanity with the final message from God. The message in the Quran and the teachings of Prophet Muhammad are not just for the Arabs into whose community Prophet Muhammad was born. The last message is from God to every human being—it's not only for existing Muslims or only for Arabs or only for people from "over there." Any believer of previously revealed scripture should make a study to determine for themselves the authenticity of Muhammad's claim to prophethood. As I discuss in the book, Jews and Christians knew there was another prophet coming...and from Arabia.

Many Westerners have indeed made such a study and have become Muslim. But it's rare that a formerly Christian woman who becomes Muslim and wears a headscarf is recognized as a native-born citizen of a Western country—most people, both Muslim and non-Muslim, assume she's Arab.

According to Muslim beliefs, Islam is the perfect code of life for all peoples in all places for all time to come. Prophet Muhammad (peace be upon him and his progeny) is a mercy for all humankind ("We did not send you but as a mercy to all the nations" Quran 21:107). "We did not send you except as a bearer of good news and warner to all mankind, but most people do not know" (Quran 34:28).

The fourth root: Guidance

Just as Jesus the Messiah (peace be upon him) was given the twelve apostles to correctly guide those who believed in the Gospel after Jesus ascended, Prophet Muhammad was given twelve vicegerents (called *imams* in Arabic). Muslims believe the apostles and vicegerents have the role of guiding humanity after the messengers from God had passed from the scene. Just like the prophets, these vicegerents were infallible.

O you who have faith! Obey Allah and obey the Apostle and those vested with authority among you. And if you dispute concerning anything, refer it to Allah and the Apostle, if you have faith in Allah and the Last Day. That is better and more favourable in outcome. (Quran 4:59)

The day We shall summon every group of people with their imam. (Quran 17:71)

-----------------------------▲-----------------------------

The twelve *imams* were all descendants of Prophet Muhammad (peace be upon him and his progeny)—not because of unwarranted nepotism but because God chose to unfold events in that manner. God tells each *imam* whom He has chosen to be the next *imam*. People do not choose for themselves. The first *imam* was Imam Ali son of Abu Talib (peace be upon him) and the twelfth (and current) one is Imam Mahdi (may God hasten his return). Imam Mahdi is descended from Simon Peter (Jesus' apostle and maternal cousin of Jesus) and Caesar of Rome on his mother's side. When Prophet Jesus (peace be upon him) returns, he and Imam Mahdi will work together to destroy the anti-christ and establish justice on Earth.

Narrations describe a moment from that era. . . Imam Mahdi is mounted on a horse and raises the flag of Prophet Muhammad. Angels come down to him—the same angels who were with Jesus when he was raised.

-----------------------------▼-----------------------------

Abu Abdullah (a) said, "It is as if I were looking at al-Qaim (a) [Imam Mahdi] outside of Najaf mounted on a horse. . . When he raises the flag of the Apostle of Allah (s) [Prophet Muhammad], thirteen thousand and thirteen angels come down to him each of whom looks to him, and they are those who were with Noah on the ark, and they were with Abraham when he was cast into the fire, and they were with Jesus at his ascension."[62]

-----------------------------▲-----------------------------

62. Mahdi Muntazir Qaim, *Jesus through Shiite Narrations,* (Qum: Ansariyan Publications). Accessed 2016
http://www.al-islam.org/jesus-though-shiite-narrations-mahdi-muntazir-qaim

The fifth root: Resurrection and judgement

The Quran teaches that there will be a point when the universe will end, a day of judgement. All of humanity will be resurrected on the Day of Judgement, and God will judge us all. We will be rewarded with one of the levels of heaven or one of the levels of hell. Islam does not teach that people go to heaven or hell as soon as they die. Rather they go to an intermediate realm where a person's spirit experiences torment or bliss similar to hell and heaven. The effects of the good deeds they have done on Earth will reach them there as people who are still alive do good deeds because of something the deceased person had done while living.

When the Imminent [Hour] befalls—there is no denying that it will befall—[it will be] lowering, exalting. When the earth is shaken violently, and the mountains are shattered into bits and become scattered dust, you will be three groups. (Quran 56:1-7)

Ten Practices of Shia Muslims

Prayer

Muslims say prayers at five required times throughout the day starting before sunrise and ending after sunset. Before saying these prayers, Muslims perform ablution (cleansing with water). They face the Kaba for the duration of the prayer—worshipping God and prostrating in submission. A Muslim may pray to God at any time throughout the day—they aren't restricted to just these five times, but praying those five prayers is required. Not all types of prayer require prostration.

Fasting

In the lunar month of Ramadan, Muslims abstain from food, drink, and sexual activity during daylight hours. Exemptions are made for those for whom fasting would cause harm. The Islamic lunar calendar is shorter than the solar calendar, so Ramadan occurs ten days sooner than the previous year every year. A Muslim may fast on just about any day during the year they prefer, but the fast in Ramadan is required for able-bodied persons of age.

Pilgrimage

Muslims are required to, at least once in a lifetime and if possible, make a pilgrimage to Mecca (*hajj*). Muslims strive to make this life-changing trip to Mecca to follow in the footsteps of Abraham and his wife Hagar. Millions of Muslims gather in this holy place to worship and to show humility and solidarity. A Muslim may make a pilgrimage to Mecca whenever they are able, but going with intention of *hajj* can only be done during a certain time period.

Wealth tax

A wealth tax (*zakah*) on certain items is required to be paid to the poor. After acquiring minimum levels of income and wealth, Muslims are required to give predefined percentages of their wealth to the needy.

Savings tax

A savings tax (*khums*) is paid on one-fifth of the increase in savings for that year after deductions.

Struggle

The greater struggle (greater *jihad*) of a Muslim is to be a good Muslim. Not every person who is a Muslim is necessarily a practicing believer—there are different levels of spirituality. Not all Muslims care about their personal struggle to righteousness—they aren't even trying and they don't care—they aren't practicing the greater struggle.

The lesser *jihad* is to defend (as in war). I talk more about that in this book.

The last of the ten practices that make up the branches of the tree are to enjoin good, to forbid evil or the prohibited, and to love God, Muhammad, Fatima (Muhammad's daughter), and the twelve imams and to reject those who terrorize them and their followers.

Appendix 2

······•◆•······

A Brief History of Islam

Islam is one of the three major world religions, along with Christianity and Buddhism. The word *islam* means harmony or peace and derives from the Arabic root *slm*—the same root as the Arabic word *salam* (peace). The word *muslim* is also derived from the Arabic root *slm*—a Muslim is one who is in complete obedience to God, one who has submitted to God.

The foremost major belief in Islam is that there is only one God. The Arabic word for the one God is *Allah*. *Allah* is a form of *al-ilah* or "the God." This word is similar to the Aramaic word *allaha* and the Hebrew word *eloha*, both meaning "God" in the singular. It is important to note that the word *Allah* is not an Islamic word but an Arabic language reference to the Creator. Christians and followers of other faiths in the Arab world call God *Allah* just as Muslims do.

Islamic belief in God is strictly monotheistic. This is different from the trinitarian or "one God in three persons" belief that a majority of Christians hold (more about that in the book). Most believing Jews are also strict monotheists, although mystical forms of Judaism (such as Kabala) are looser in this regard.

The holy scripture of Islam is the Quran. *Quran* is an Arabic word that has been translated as "the lecture" and "the message" and "the recital." The Quran was revealed in the seventh century CE to an Arab named Muhammad who is the prophet of Islam. Muhammad (peace be upon him and his progeny) considered himself a human and, therefore, a non-divine prophet. Muslims believe that he is the last prophet after 124,000 other prophets including Adam, Noah, Abraham, Isaac, Ishmael, Jacob, Joseph, Moses, Solomon, John the Baptist, and Jesus the Messiah, among many others—peace be upon them all. Prophets were sent to their peoples to preach obedience to God by turning to God and away from sinful ways.

Originally, Arabs (descending from Prophet Ishmael) worshipped God. Their holy sanctuary was the Kaba[63] in Mecca in Western Arabia. Eventually, the majority of Arabs turned away from monotheism and began worshipping man-made idols. Various tribes would come to Mecca every year on pilgrimage and worship the idols in the Kaba. Jews and Christians (People of the Book[64]) settled in Western Arabia. Some Arabs became Christians, though most continued to worship their idols.

In the early seventh century CE, Muhammad (peace be upon him and his progeny) was called by God to be the prophet to all people, including Arabs, his own people. Furthermore, Muhammad was to be the last prophet sent by God, and so the message of Islam was sent to the Byzantine and Sassanid (Persian) emperors and to other nations through emissaries sent to them by Prophet Muhammad.

At first, Muslims worshipped in private. Soon it became time to tell the Arabs of Mecca about Islam. Some of the practices of the Arabs that Muhammad preached against were polytheism, treating women as mere property, burying unwanted female infants alive, slavery, mistreating or not helping the poor, and tribal warfare.

The Meccan rulers responded by persecuting the Muslims. Some Muslims were sent to live under the safety of the king of Ethiopia where

---

63. A building at the center of Masjid al-Haram Mosque in Mecca, Saudi Arabia; first built by angels for Adam and Eve and restored by Abraham and Ishmael
64. In the Quran this term is used for those people who worship God and to whom were sent prophets and who had scriptures.

Muslims successfully made their case against agents of the Meccan rulers who wanted to bring them back to Mecca. Eventually, the city of Yathrib, where some of the citizens had believed Muhammad's message, invited Muhammad to lead them because of their internal conflicts. Thus, the first Islamic state was born. Muslims who were able fled to Yathrib, now called the City (of the Prophet) or Medina. The Meccan rulers attempted to murder the Prophet in his bed, but the Prophet managed to escape to Medina. His cousin, Ali, stayed in the Prophet's bed as a decoy, risking his life. When the assassins saw that it was Ali, they did not carry out the attack.

The Muslims of Medina were called the "helpers" while the Muslims who came from Mecca were called the "immigrants." The Meccan rulers attempted to destroy the Muslims' community. The first major battle (Battle of Badr) was a victory for Muslims. The second major battle (Battle of Uhud) should have been a victory also, but some archers abandoned their position to get their share of the booty leaving the flank indefensible. The Prophet was almost killed in this attack. The third major battle (Battle of the Trench) was fought when Mecca attacked Medina. The Muslims built a trench to protect the city, but a traitor in their midst left an area unprotected. Nevertheless, the battle was ultimately won by the Muslims, and Medina was saved.

Muhammad was now able to make a treaty with the Meccans who appeared to be unfavorable toward the Muslims. This allowed the Muslims to make their pilgrimage to Mecca during the following year and allowed Muslims to send teachers to other Arab tribes producing many converts to Islam. Allies of Mecca broke the treaty after a few years, and the Muslims marched to and captured Mecca bloodlessly, as several of the Meccan leaders themselves declared they had become Muslims. Eventually, all of Arabia became a united Islamic community.

89269037R00081

Made in the USA
Lexington, KY
25 May 2018